ROOMS OF THE
MIND

ROOMS OF THE
MIND

Quadrants for Success

TERRY M. BROWN, Ed.D.

outskirts
press

Outskirts Press, Inc.
http://www.outskirtspress.com

ISBN: 978-1-4327-5512-6

Outskirts Press and the "OP" logo are trademarks belonging to Outskirts Press, Inc.

PRINTED IN THE UNITED STATES OF AMERICA

Contents

CHAPTER 1

Role of Policy Makers

One certainty exists in the United States: public schools across the nation have the daunting task each year of providing children with a first-rate education. The immediate question to ponder is: Will the provision of the highest quality of education for school-children who are the nation's future become a national priority? Appropriate questions to be considered when children enter the formal education process are: Who in the educational system is responsible for capturing and connecting the child's mind to the learning process that is required for success in American schools? Are teachers, principals, or policymakers responsible for inspiring schoolchildren to learn, or do children bear most of the responsibility for their success or failure in American schools?

Despite inherent beliefs regarding compulsory education for school-aged children, the Constitution of the United States does not mandate that children attend school. No statement, clause, statute, or amendment exists in the United States Constitution authorizing children to attend public or private school. Unlike the role other levels of government play in establishing and regulating schools, the role that the federal government plays in educating children in the United States is less than that of the state or local role in education. The federal government enjoys only those powers conferred or reasonably implied by the U. S. Constitution, and this document makes no mention of education (Webb, McCarthy, Thomas, 1988).

Considering the fact that the thirteen original colonies were occupied in the Revolutionary War to secure the nation's independence, education was not the important issue in the formulation of the nation's constitution. The forefathers crafted the Constitution as a basis for the nation's legal system. They were primarily concerned with establishing a document that provided order in society, one that helped to resolve disputes and protect its people and property. Formal education for children, however, existed within the colonies and was quite important to the early settlers. The education of children in the colonies was essentially based on a family's structure and its standing within the community.

> The colonists' conception of institutionalized education was decidedly centered on social class. The children of workers and peasants should have a minimum primary education, in vernacular schools, to learn reading, writing, arithmetic, and religion. While the lower-class children were to have only a few years of primary schooling, the male offspring of the middle and upper classes would attend the Latin Grammar school, a college preparatory institution, and then go on to college. Thus, the colonists believed in a two-track system of schools: one for the poor and another for the wealthy. (Gutek, 1988)

The federal government's role in directing a child's prescribed education is minimal at best. A national educational system that incorporates precise curricular and instructional priorities for educating children does not exist in the United States. Educating children in this country has essentially been relegated to individual states since the formulation of the compulsory educational system.

One explanation for the disparities in the academic achievement of school-aged children across the nation may be found in the organization of each state's educational system.

A number of state legislatures set educational laws requiring the state's highest educational governing body, usually some form of a state board of education, to administer and enforce the educational laws of the state. State boards of education maintain authority and jurisdiction over the essential aspects of the state's educational system. They regulate elementary and secondary educational systems and manage state departments of instruction and local boards of education located within their jurisdiction. The state board of education oversees a wide and comprehensive range of educational functions including courses of study, the school calendar, student textbooks, transportation, alternative education, nutritional and media services. The state board of education establishes the legal authority of local school board members and stipulates the duties of superintendents, supervisors, principals, teachers, and other school employees in the state's school districts.

Local boards of education are authorized to develop school policies that comply with state laws and indicate how the education of children is to be regulated and carried out in the local school district, parish, city, county, or municipality. The local board of education retains the services of a schools superintendent who supervises the local educational system and is charged with developing curricular and school policies for the school district. The school principals, teachers, and staff must execute the plans instituted by the superintendent and approved by the local board of education. The superintendent's strategies for academic improvement within the school district, whether the plans are academic or managerial, must be directed toward how children learn and aimed at the overall improvement of all aspects of the educational system.

Uniformity across school districts with reference to the improvement of a child's education does not exist, nor does the standardization of academic development across states. Local boards of education are to be commended for being the front runners in improving academic achievement in American schools and for instituting policies that have governed education in past years. Yet there are literally thousands of local boards of education in the United States generating virtually thousands of different ways children are educated. Over 15,000 local school boards meet regularly to provide policy guidance for U.S. education (First, 1992).

In American schools standardized guidelines for how, what, and when schoolchildren learn are nonexistent. The only guiding principle is that each child should receive at best a basic education. A typical basic education consists of developing reading, writing, and computational skills in the primary grades. However, there are no specific national agreements on how those skills are to be taught to schoolchildren. In secondary grades a set number of courses are established in order for students to obtain a diploma. That, essentially, is how schools across the United States organize to educate the nation's youth. In essence, what and how a child learns in school are based more on local decisions than decisions made for the entire state. Educational uniformity at both levels of education, elementary and secondary, is missing from top to bottom in schools across the country.

The standard American school calendar dates back to 1852, when the first compulsory attendance laws were enacted, requiring students to attend school for twelve weeks during the school year (Maine Task Force Report, 1994). In 1890, the average, public school year had increased to the present-day thirty-six weeks of instruction. Traditional American school calendars allot time for study uniformly and consistently in school districts from state to state.

Each student is expected to spend roughly the same number of hours in school, complete the same number of courses and attend school for the same number of years. The National Center for Educational Statistics listed the average number of days in the school year for American elementary and secondary students at 178 (Dlugosh, 1994). Compared to the first compulsory attendance laws, students in the first quarter of the 21st century attended school more often. In 1852 students were out of school for forty of the fifty-two weeks of the Gregorian calendar year. Under the present compulsory attendance laws students are out of school sixteen weeks in the summer months.

Some state legislatures set minimum standards for school calendars. According to the National Commission on Time and Learning (1993), most states require 175 to 180 days of instruction in the academic school year. However, state policies vary on the length of the school day by grade level. Some state legislatures give local boards of education authority over the length of the school day and year for their schoolchildren. In some cases state legislatures set the time and day public schools are to open and close.

Local boards of education adopt school calendars that are supportive of community needs and educational programs established in the school district that those boards of education serve. The majority of American school calendars operate concurrently with three of the four seasons of the Gregorian calendar. In most states that operate on traditional school calendars, students are out of school nearly all of the months of June, July, and August. Time spent away from school during the summer months does not benefit some students and may be detrimental to retaining information learned during the preceding school year. The New York Board of Regents (1992) found that students who are above grade level continue to learn during the summer months primarily because of the efforts of parents to provide enrichment activities or experiences outside the formal learning environment.

The study reported that educationally advantaged students, or students whose parents could afford to place them in summer enrichment activities, gained an average of one additional month's growth in the summer. Educationally disadvantaged students or students who were educationally inactive during the summer months were likely to lose three to four months of growth from their gains of the previous school year. The effect of this learning loss for the two groups of students, after seven years of school, was that the advantaged students scored at the ninth-grade plus level in school, whereas the educationally disadvantaged students scored at the fourth to fifth grade level (New York Board of Regents, 1992).

School districts have been encouraged to discover supplementary methods to keep their school doors open throughout the Gregorian calendar year. The school clock, as well as the calendar, has governed how schools cover material during the traditional school year. To become successful students must be given ample time and opportunity to comprehend and master the information that is presented to them. More appropriate and suitable methods of increasing time are needed in the public-school calendar to challenge students as they journey through the twenty-first century. Education has always been and must continue to be the United States' first line of defense because as the nation progresses, it can only maintain its present status by educating its youth better than yesterday's generation. Education in American schools needs reform because an increasing number of students are not mastering the essential curriculum (Wiebe, 1992).

Students who attend school on the traditional calendar do not benefit from 180 days of instruction. Primarily because of their long absences from the school environment during the summer months, teachers at the beginning of each school year spend considerable time reviewing, examining and appraising learning loss. Teachers also devote considerable time at the beginning of the school year attending to classroom management and procedural activities relating to school rules and regulations. Classroom time devoted to managerial details at the beginning of the traditional school year is necessary, though there are more important concerns such as academic instruction. Finding the time in the school calendar to promote equitable curricular standards may prove to be sound practice in an era when American students are falling further behind students in other developed countries around the world.

The National Commission on Excellence in Education reported that American students ranked last out of nineteen achievement tests when compared to international students. Students in America continue to fall further behind students in developed countries in basic literacy. From 1969 to 1989, American students slipped from first to forty-ninth among 148 nations in basic literacy (Daggett, 1990). Daggett reported that much was done in the form of initiating reforms in the 1980s, and educators should be applauded for their efforts. However, students have little to show academically for the labor that was exerted. Daggett wrote that the school systems across the United States had failed students miserably.

European and Asian students enjoy an increasingly higher level of academic achievement over American students. According to the National Center for Education Statistics, reading scores in America have changed only minimally since the early 1970s (Reichmann, 1995). Students in many countries abroad attend school for more days than American students (Beck, 1992). In elementary school American students spend less time engaged in actual academic activities than Chinese and Japanese students. The National Commission on Time and Learning (1993) reported that the average number of days students attend United States schools ranked ninth out of ten countries. The National Commission on Time and Learning reports that Japan leads the world in the average number of days students spend in school each year.

The difference in the number of days American students are required to attend school (178 days) and the average number of days Japanese students attend school (240 days) may be part of the reason Japanese students outperform American students.

In a study of ten countries including England, Canada, France, Germany, Israel, Japan, New Zealand, South Korea, and Taiwan, the United States was below average in the number of days students attend school.

Where is the urgency in the American educational system to impel students to become top performers in the competitive world? Where does the arrow of complacency in American public schools point, as students continue to fall further behind students in other developed countries? What has happened to the U.S. competitive educational spirit since the launching of Sputnik sparked a national urge to improve achievements in mathematics and science in schools across the country? Who is responsible for opening the doors that lead to the rooms of the mind where learning takes place?

The strong educational fibers that made this nation great seem to be eroding, washed away by long-standing complacency in present-day American schools. Weak attitudes about education have no boundaries or limits and cast a dark shadow on the educational future of the country. Programs and reforms initiated to plug the leaks and stop the rising tide of mediocrity in the educational system have not worked for all students. There must be insistence, determination, and a rush to revitalize and improve student learning in schools across the nation if American students are to regain the top educational position in the world as measured by standardized achievement tests.

Educators must remain committed and willing to stand by principles that allow all students the opportunity to learn, to grow academically and develop fully as productive U.S. citizens. The nation can no longer stand by, watching from a distance, as generations of American children fall further behind other students in developed countries. What must happen to alter the course on which education is presently headed?

The last century ushered in the excellence-in-education movement in the United States. Historically, a strong emphasis was placed on educational achievement through programs, reforms, and initiatives. Hass and Parkay (1993) chronicled that century's educational events: (a) Committee of Ten, (b) Sputnik's emphasis on mathematics and science, (c) A Nation at Risk, (d) Carnegie Council on Adolescent Development, (e) President George H. Bush's Goals 2000, and (f) President Bill Clinton's Ten Point Plan for change. The first quarter of the third millennium has seen the move toward student learning through other school focused initiatives: President George W. Bush's No Child Left Behind initiative, President Barack Obama's Reforming Education through Race to the Top, President Donald J. Trump's Executive Order 13791, and President Joseph R. Biden, Jr.'s Bipartisan Safer Communities Act. Given the minimal effect that the federal government has on education, what will be the impact, and how will education transform student achievement in the second quarter of the third millennium?

All of the initiatives that were set forth in the last century suggest that curriculum, instruction, and assessment must be more challenging if American schools are to prepare their students to compete globally. State and local bodies that govern schools must not show a reluctance to enact practical, school-policy approaches to student learning that ensure continued trends to excellence in education. It has been suggested that there should be more effective instruction in schools because of the way traditional schools have distributed learning time within the school year. School reforms have been designed to deliberately change people, school systems, and the organizational cultures in which people operate, while keeping yesterday's model operating until the switch that activates the new model can be turned on (Lezotte, 1994).

CHAPTER 2

Role of the School District

A school community should insist that its school district facilitate curricular and academic improvements for all children enrolled in schools within the district. School leaders are charged with providing students enrolled in their school district the best education possible. The success or failure of education reforms in public school districts are a direct reflection of the programs and policies implemented by curriculum leaders. Educational policy makers need better data to ascertain how policy implementation and reforms affects the lack of student achievement.

The challenge of improving education should be taken up by educational professionals who have firsthand knowledge of curriculum and instruction (Elmore and Fuhrman, 1994). To construct systemic changes and encourage positive advances in academics school districts must chart and coordinate professional development for all of the district's staff.

Professional development should be provided for teachers, teacher assistants, principals, supervisors and the superintendent's staff. A well-structured, professional development program is the basis of broad-based employee improvement within a school district. Professional development opportunities augment a teacher's knowledge and understanding of how children learn. John Dewey (1966) established that certainty is an essential property of anything entitled to be called knowledge. An educator's knowledge of curriculum, instruction, and assessment develops strength bands when it is presented with staff development opportunities. Expanded professional development opportunities for school employees, whether at the school or district level, produce knowledgeable curriculum leaders. Professional development plans assist school-district leaders by familiarizing employees with individual school or district curriculum initiatives. Staff development provides experienced teachers with an opportunity to mentor inexperienced teachers based on the curricular, instructional, or appraisal requirements instituted within the school or the school district.

A curriculum comprises all the planned learning outcomes for which a school is responsible (Oliva, 1988). A curriculum is a printed course of study, subject matter, course content, and planned experiences or activities within the confines of the school and extends beyond the school's boundaries. The school district's curriculum serves as a teachers' guide to the decision-making process. Curricular results help district leaders determine whether schools and school districts are maximizing learning for their schoolchildren. Vast variations in cognitive processing exist between children at various educational growth levels. Making these levels explicit has the major advantage of forcing the teacher to identify and develop the kind of instructional activities that teach these processes and the test items that provide evidence of a student's performance level (Gentile, 1988). To help students move successfully through stratified learning levels, teachers must decide if the students needs additional time to learn, more suitable resources that refocus them on previously taught concepts, or more advanced levels of instruction.

Schools are jam packed with masses of extrinsically and intrinsically motivated children who must be pushed by educators to learn the essential curriculum developed by curriculum leaders. Good teaching involves assessing whether students are absorbed in the lesson and learning what is being taught. Recognition of the differences between individual schoolchildren is central to teacher effectiveness. Educators must determine how children process information and provide alternative learning paths for them. Teachers must ascertain which kinds of knowledge have the most value, determine individual differences and provide inspiration in the learning process. Curriculum leaders, school and district personnel must serve as the catalyst for curriculum development. Curriculum leaders must relay and communicate to teachers the role that the curriculum plays in the learning process and its benefits. The school principal must encourage teachers to deliver the curriculum more effectively and lend a hand in helping classroom teachers to reach their fullest potential.

To increase their students' engagement in the learning process, teachers must move away from the desk or lectern and reposition themselves nearer their students. Elevating a student's level of concern causes the student to be motivated. Learners are motivated to do that which concerns them. You cannot motivate a learner, but you can arrange conditions to increase the probability that the motivation to learn will become stronger (Hunter, 1982). Public-school curriculum leaders are required to assess standards of learning and information considered worth learning.

Classroom teachers, when faced with circumstances related to student values, are required to use the school district policies that outline character traits or student responsibility. However, teachers should have confidence in their own educational philosophy as it relates to influencing or determining students' educational choices. Children learn at an early age that success usually brings awards or rewards. The idea is embedded in the structure of our schools (Webb, 1981). Since educational excellence for children is the goal, successful academic attainment should be dependent on the decisions of curriculum planners and teachers.

When developing goals and objectives, curriculum leaders must convey theoretical instructions to educators who need ideas that focus on student achievement. Curriculum leaders have to bridge the gap between teaching and learning by linking theory and practice in curriculum development. School systems respond to public pressure and to state departments of public instruction that set objectives and criteria for curricular improvements in schools and school systems. They must acknowledge that educational reforms and philosophies should steer curricular decisions. School systems generally are well-informed organizations and stay up to date on information about educational theories and philosophies. School systems understand that educational reforms and philosophies drive curricular decisions. However, to truly advance academic achievement, school district curriculum leaders must move beyond theories of learning and focus on practical learning applications.

School curriculum developers must not tolerate or allow instability in the curriculum. Therefore they must examine more than test scores to make decisions about student learning. District leaders should think about children in the framework of the entire educational plan including the emotional and physical development of a child as well as a child's mental development. Teachers are obligated to practice what works for children. It is critical that teachers focus on the child and let effective instructional methods guide and drive curricular decisions. Students fail to learn when they are disconnected from the classroom teacher and the learning process. The teacher must check to make sure the learner has heard the correct information (Hunter, 1982). The disengaged student must persistently be reunited with the teacher and lessons taught by that teacher to eliminate further disparities in learning. That is the ultimate responsibility of a classroom teacher.

When schools or school systems lack sufficient resources to carry out plans for educational improvement curriculum planners should postpone plans until resources become available. The rationale for long-term planning requires commitments from stakeholders to collect staff input, retrieve strategic data, solve issues that may hinder improvement within the system and devise a plan of action for the progress of the school or school district. What are the systemic problems that obstruct improvement within the school or school district? Where are the academic deficiencies located within the school organizational design? Are the challenges of improving achievement in schools to be found at the planning stage? Are they at the developmental level, or are the imperfections to be found at the implementation phase? What are the strengths of the school or school system and how will the school or school district accomplish the acknowledged goal? After intervention, how long will it take before academic progress shows improved results? The curricular plan should reflect the steps needed to improve student academic achievement in the school district. The curriculum plan must hold superintendents answerable for school-district improvements in academic achievement. School principals must be held responsible for visible results in the educational achievement and teachers must be held responsible for escalating educational improvement at the classroom level. The plan should challenge students to perform at higher levels of learning with the understanding that the end result may be increased student achievement.

If effective principals become risk takers, successful teachers should also take risks in the classroom. Effective teachers know how to teach and are the educational specialists on whom children, parents, principals, and the school district rely to improve student achievement. Teachers anticipate principals visiting their classroom and providing instructional assistance on their teaching performance. School principals have an obligation to present teachers with feedback that will assist them in developing into efficient and effective teachers.

The school district and the school must arrange for all teachers to have total access to educational improvement goals. Principals are responsible for teachers' knowledge of district goals and for teachers' proficiency at disseminating district objectives to their students. School principals must make sure that teachers know and understand school goals and comprehend the school district's learning objectives. It is meaningful and beneficial to student success when teachers share ideas and information that have been successful for the educational level at which they teach. Instructional leaders who impart high-quality ideas to other teachers are ideal examples of learning facilitators.

An old axiom asserts that where there is smoke, there must be fire. In a lot of cases a fire may exist, but only the smoke can be seen. A burning building emits smoke high into the clouds, which can be seen from afar. The viewer may deduce that a fire exists somewhere although it cannot be seen. Could the same argument be made for curriculum and instruction? Where there is instruction in the classroom, a curriculum must be present; where there exists a curriculum in the school, there must be instruction.

Oliva (1988) identified curriculum as that which is taught and instruction as the means used to teach that which is taught. Curriculum is classified as *what* teachers instruct and instruction is *how* teachers deliver the lesson. Curriculum is a syllabus, a strategy, a course, a proposal, a design, a scheme, and a planned road map for student learning. Instruction, on the other hand, embodies the teacher's methods and techniques, the behavior of the teacher, execution of the school or district plan, or the manner of address. A teacher is observed instructing children during the school day. Can the observer deduce that the teacher is instructing from a planned curriculum although a curriculum cannot be seen? Is it possible to separate the curriculum from instruction? They may be recognized as two entities, but like Siamese twins who are joined together, one may not function without the other (Oliva, 1988).

The task of teaching schoolchildren requires the teacher to serve as the catalyst for student learning. Teaching means channeling a developing child to learn and requires that the teacher and student perform specific activities during the lesson. Reason, intuition, analysis, insight, perception, and observation form the foundation of learning. A theory of learning is not a theory of instruction. To learn, the student must be receptive. The teacher, on the other hand, controls the activity that propels the child's learning. Professional educators who are responsible for developing theories of learning and enabling instructional practices to be used in classroom situations, recognize that theory and practice are unified aspects of teaching. Without guiding principles, teachers only have a miniscule chance of being successful. Successful teachers frequently base their decisions on established research.

Some compelling theories of learning suggest that optimum structuring of knowledge, sequential learning, pacing, and student rewards sometimes play critical roles in learning. Effective instruction requires a teacher to have an elevated awareness, and it encourages open-mindedness that tends to generate and guide teaching behaviors and promote a system for student feedback.

A curriculum should be determined by the subject's fundamental structure (Bruner, 1963). When children learn the structure of a subject, they begin to understand how things are related and the subject becomes comprehendible. Structure improves their memory, and allows them to grasp the details of ideas and conceptual patterns. They can transfer this understanding of fundamental structure to similar curricula. Bruner refers to the structure of a subject as basic ideas or fundamental principles.

To learn the structure of a subject is to understand it in such a way that it permits other subjects to be meaningfully related. Learning takes place through the learner's experiences and reactions to his or her environment. The learning experience is the interaction between the learner and the environment. Learning takes place through the actions of the learner. It is what the student does rather than what the teacher does.

Two students, when placed together in the same class, experience different stimuli from the teacher. One student follows the teacher's instructions and is totally submerged and interested in the lesson. That student connects with the teacher and structures knowledge received from the lesson. The other student is disengaged from the teacher and the lesson, devotes class time and attention to planning for an after-school activity and does not connect with the teacher or the lesson. It is obvious that although the two students are in the same class, they do not have the same educational experience. Bruner theorized that children benefit from learning experiences through their own discoveries. Discovery means the learner must become an active participant in the class and be attracted to features of the environment. The learner must at some time become intrinsically motivated to reach his or her fullest potential in the learning process.

The teacher provides the educational experience by setting up an environment and structuring classroom lessons so that students reach the goals desired by the teacher. The teacher must understand the student's interests and set up a meaningful learning experience for that student. Children learn best when the material meets a recognized need rather than being forced to memorize it (Kilpatrick, 1941). Kilpatrick believed that children need contact with concrete objects, places, and people, which they do with books and other printed materials, and the school should be concerned with developing the whole child.

Part of the responsibility for shaping students' minds rests with curriculum leaders who are responsible for providing curriculum activities that stimulate students. To reach their intellectual capacity students must find a balance between external and internal stimuli. When appealing to children, teachers must prove they are qualified to do so by arousing the children's enthusiasm and directing their emotions toward the action to be taken (Adler, 1983). Adler wrote that teachers cannot bring motivating passions into play in a classroom until they have aroused favorable feelings in their students. There is little point in resorting to reason and argument if the teacher has not established a receptive atmosphere.

CHAPTER 3

School Organization

Public schools are structured institutions in which a number of members in the organization perform specific tasks designed to cultivate the minds and bodies of children assigned to the organization by the school district. In school organizations, unlike most organizations, the student is required to be admitted into the organization regardless of whether they want to be in school or not. In fact, attendance in school is monitored and enforced by the organization. It is mandatory that American children who have reached the age of five or six be admitted into public schools. In most organizations an individual must apply to become a member and after applying for admission into the organization, the individual must be accepted into the organization by the leader(s) or committees representing the organization. The individual may or may not be approved for entrance into the organization. An individual must apply and be approved for membership into Masonic Groups, into colleges and universities, fraternities and sororities, for employment into businesses, for military service, to own a professional sports team, for medical school, law school, and graduate school, and parents must apply for their child to be admitted into a private school.

Organizations are rarely established as ends in themselves. They are instruments created to achieve other ends. This is reflected in the origins of the word *organization*, meaning a tool or instrument. It is therefore no wonder that those ideas about tasks, goals, aims, and objectives have become fundamental organizational concepts (Morgan, 1986). In American schools the employees are the critical resource that helps children succeeds each year. Therefore school employees are the most important assets in the organization. School board members and school superintendents must make the improvement of employee caliber its highest priority. As school employees become more educated in the workforce they want to exert more influence on the decisions that govern their work with children.

Contributive approaches to managing schools should put most of the decision making, information, knowledge, power, and rewards in the hands of the teachers. A highly educated and effective instructional workforce demands a say in the day-to-day work activities and decisions that govern the development of schoolchildren. Highly productive, contributive school employees feel that they are entitled to better wages, benefits, and working conditions. Employee participation can significantly improve the organization's effectiveness (Lawler, 1986). The degree to which school employees contribute to the organization's functions is reflected in the organization's effectiveness.

If teachers feel that the school organization creates opportunities for personal growth, they will commit more time and energy into making schools more productive. On the other hand, when teachers perceive that the school organization is autocratic and impersonal, they may not buy into the goals of that organization. The approach that school organizations take to decisions related to teachers determines the willingness of the teachers to accept the district's educational methods and ideas.

The move toward more employee participation has resulted in the formation of many kinds of decision-making work teams. These teams are chartered, among other things, to improve quality, increase efficiency, and strive for total customer satisfaction.

Employees are asked to do things they have not done before, and their leaders are asked to try new ways of managing (Rees, 1991). The traditional apex-down style organization, which is led by school administrators who make all the decisions and control teachers leads to organizational disassociation by teachers. They view autocratic management as organization centered and they do not see opportunities to be rewarded for contributions they make within the organization. Rewards are an important consideration in school organizations and teachers become highly motivated when they feel that they will be rewarded for their actions. Teachers will make reasonable decisions to expend more time and energy in the organization if they view the organization as favorable.

Lawler states that individuals must see connections between their performance in the organization and rewards if the organization expects employees to increase productivity. If teachers distance themselves from the organization, it is an indication that they do not see reward opportunities. How do school organizations persuade their employees to accept the goals and objectives set forth for school improvement and induce teachers to work to their fullest potential to make their organizations successful? What is it about the school work place that persuades teachers to work more productively? How does a school organization reward its teachers for the work that they do? When school organizations grant teachers the chance to provide input in the decisions that are made for student improvement the process becomes positive and productive for teachers and the organization.

Teachers in school organizations, when given opportunities to make decisions about student learning, propose concrete learning ideas and when given a chance to discuss issues about curriculum, instruction and assessment, see a shift in communication from an authoritarian organization to an employee contributive organization. The flow of information is crucial in determining how effectively the school system meets the challenges teachers face in the organization. If school organizations are to remain effective, it is critical that certain types of information be accessible to teachers. Employee effectiveness depends on a flawless flow of information between school administrators and teachers. School administrators must steer information that teachers provide in the direction the school organization wants to go for the most effective development of their students.

By and large, schools are organized around three major educational components: curriculum, instruction, and assessment. Increasingly, however, student assessment has nudged its way to become the key component in the teaching and learning process. Assessment has progressively become the educational spotlight that shines on student achievement in schools today. State and federally mandated assessment of public schoolchildren became a passionately debated issue in public-school education at the onset of the twenty-first century. Are schools in America at a point where district, state, and federal demands for the assessment of students overshadow curriculum and instruction? Students have always been tested in schools. It is a part of the fiber of the schooling process. Assessment of educational progress has and forever will be necessary to accurately measure a student's academic progress. Testing and assessing students, however, should not become an instrument for diminishing the importance of curriculum and instruction in the learning process.

In so far as education is concerned, there must remain a wholesome balance between the key elements of curriculum, instruction, and assessment and the three sides of the triangle must remain reasonable and equivalent. The lines that connect the educational triangle must remain equilateral at all times rather than isosceles or scalene in nature. The ability to keep the lines of the educational triangle equal in scope is similar to the checks and balances system of the three branches of government: the executive, judicial, and legislative. The three branches of government monitor each other so that one branch of government does not become more powerful than another. So it is in the educational arena: one leg of the educational process should not overpower another leg of the educational system.

In the three legs of the educational triangle, the student curriculum is relinquished by the curriculum developers and given to the teachers charged with instructing students who are assessed to see what they have learned. District leaders purposefully select curricula that benefit the children enrolled in their schools and charge school teachers with delivering instruction. Teachers administer tests to students to evaluate how well they have mastered or learned a given curriculum. The three lines of the educational triangle: curriculum, instruction, and assessment have been used in schools since the concept of the one-room schoolhouse.

Assessment of children in the twenty-first century is much more competitive than the latter years of the twentieth century when mandated state and federal accountability standards were established. Assessment in the present day compares one student's achievement against another student's achievement, and one teacher's scores against another teacher's scores. It compares one grade-level score against another grade-level score, one school's achievement against another school's achievement, one school district's scores against another school district's scores, one state's achievement results against another state's achievement, and one developed nation's scores against another developed nation's scores. The degree to which student achievement scores are compared has changed the curricular, instructional, and assessment landscape.

Accountability in school organizations requires that communities pressure school boards, school boards pressure superintendents, superintendent's pressure principals, and principals pressure teachers to improve student achievement. One example of how student assessment has evolved and impacted teachers occurred at my school. At the end of each grading period teachers were required to administer assessments and provide students and parents with a progress report on the objectives and goals that were taught during the assessment timeframe. All teachers who failed students at 5 percent or greater (total class population) were required to provide me with modifications to correct the failures. The 5 percent student failure rule was based in part on my philosophical indoctrination during a professional development activity focused on curriculum alignment that took place in the period between my last year as a public school teacher and first year as a school administrator. A statement of student learning crafted by the educators at the workshop had a profound effect on my educational philosophy of student improvement. After the workshop, the seminar educators were required to disseminate the statement to the staff at all schools in the school district. The statement that arose from the workshop was worded as follows:

> An effective school is a school where 95 percent or more of the children, without regard to race, color, creed, origin, nationality, gender, ethnic background, religion, culture, or primary language, master the essential curriculum at every grade level and every content area, which will be made evident on nationally standardized tests and other outcomes over a period of three to five years. (Tony Monihan McCoy, 1991)

Although the 95 percent rule was evoked at the school where I was principal, it is my belief that 100 percent of the students under the instructional care of a teacher should be accounted for at all times during each evaluation period. On the assessment instrument, three questions were asked of teachers failing 5 percent or more students during a grading period:

1. What are the instructional changes that you will consider

in order to increase student achievement with the children that you teach by the end of the next reporting period?

This question asks teachers precisely how they plan to change instruction to decrease the number of failures by the next grading period.

2. What instructional strategies will you use to improve student achievement by the end of the next reporting period?

   This question asks teachers to list the strategies that they will use in the subsequent grading period and that are different from the preceding grading period. How would changes be made to decrease failures by the next assessment period?

3. What resources will you need to facilitate improved student achievement in the next instructional period?

   This asks teachers how the principal can assist them with the instructional resources they need to decrease the number of failures.

After meeting with me to discuss the number of failures for the grading period, each teacher was required to develop a plan of action and give me an instructional assessment plan prior to the first day of the new reporting period. The instructional assessment plan, written by the teacher, proposed additional strategies for correcting the failures of each child under the 5 percent rule. It also stressed continued improvements in students who achieved an acceptable degree of improvement during the grading period. The success or failure of the instructional assessment plan was evaluated by me throughout the duration of the grading period and at the conclusion of the instructional period.

Each year, as principals analyze school test scores, the contingency theory determines the results of the test scores for the school year and dictates principals' interactions with teachers. As task-oriented behavior is imposed on schools nationwide, student testing will invariably increase the burden on district leaders, principals, teachers, and students to improve test scores each school year. What effect does an increased ultimatum for improved test scores have on students' and teachers' abilities to produce satisfactory tests scores? One outcome seems certain as schools move through the twenty-first century, public school principals will evolve into situational leaders, bound more by task behavior than relationship behavior partly because of greater demands for improved testing and accountability standards. Public-school principals and teachers should employ monitoring tactics that measure student academic progress as the school year progresses. Incrementally measured academic assessments of student progress throughout the school year allow principals, teachers the advantage of working to improve students' weaknesses and augment students' strengths prior to state-mandated achievement tests at the end of each school year.

Based on the climate at the school and the students' end-of-year assessment results, school principals must make changes where needed. In schools where test scores are constantly under scrutiny principals may view circumstances associated with assessment as more related to accomplishing a particular set of tasks than to forming relationships with the staff. To motivate teachers and students to accomplish assessment goals, the principal adapts to testing and assessment situations rather than to establishing relationships with the teachers. When a school principal receives the end-of-year, mandated state or local test results, regardless of whether the results are positive or negative, the final results of the tests have proven to be the greatest initiator of situational leadership for school principals. If the final assessment results fail to meet the goals and objectives set by the principal and teachers at the beginning of the school year, the situation calls for in-depth analysis of how to improve students' tests scores in the next school year. Relationships with teachers may become strained because teachers will constantly be challenged to change their testing strategies and do more for their students the next school year. Principals will be challenged to find ways to raise student achievement to a respectable standard in the school district.

A poem referencing how mandated testing in public schools has impacted school staffs and communities across the United States was introduced to the faculty and staff by the school principal at the start of the new academic year. The student assessment poem was written for returning and new teachers but was shared with the school staff prior to the students' return from summer vacation. Before sharing the poem with the staff, the principal discussed the results of the assessment of the preceding school year. "Climb Every Mountain" by Rodgers and Hammerstein played in the background as the poem was read to the staff during the meeting.

A Test of Will

At the end of nine school months of the calendar year
Schools in states across America
Prepare students for one immense week of testing.
The final state tests of mandated subjects,
Every phase of a school's instructional operations
Are focused on one single goal during the school year:
Preparing its students to pass the state tests
Millions of students take state tests each year.
The tests represent the state's accountability system.
The upmost test of will for students,
One successful year of tests scores,
Can boost a school's image for years to come.
The stakes are high, but the rewards are great.
High achieving schools receive the state's best accolades.
All across the nation people watch for and read
Stories of its schools' successes in newspapers and on TV,
Watching to see which schools emerged as high achievers.

Testing children has become the nation's
Hottest pressure cooker in schools today.
Each year has its share of students
Who pass the tests with impressive statistics.
The end-of-year tests have become legendary
And are made up of stories, successes, and failures.
Each year brings new conquests and groups of students
Willing to tackle and conquer the state tests.
Each year the state tests are blown apart and analyzed,
Clearing the path for and searching for the schools
That made their way to the top.
Successful school achievement is celebrated.
Unproductive schools face inquiry for failing.
After all is said and done and a new year begins
Principals and teachers fire up the testing process again,
Expecting to have success in the new school year

Schools are educational institutions where elements of learning, through teachers, come together for students, and schools operate as a home away from home for students during the school day. Schools exist to develop a student's mind and body, to teach subject content, and to produce inquiring, thinking individuals. Public schools expect students to become more knowledgeable and adept at learning content and to continue to develop and prosper as outstanding students throughout the learning process. All children, according to Dewey (1966), are destined for leisure and learning as well as for labor. All have the same three elements in their futures: the demands of work, the duties of citizenship, and the obligation of each individual to make the most of his or her capacities to lead rich and fulfilling lives (Adler, 1984). The instructional plan established by district leaders must be targeted toward increased student achievement within the school district. How is the instructional plan organized? How does student learning affect the development and implementation of the instructional plan? Does the instructional plan meet the needs of the students? School principals have an obligation to be instructional leaders, to mobilize resources for the school staff, and direct teacher involvement in the instructional process.

The school principal ought to consider using as many as possible of the school's parents, community, and businesses leaders as resources to help the school achieve its goals and objectives for school improvement. The principal should make contact with community leaders for assistance in shaping the school's curricular and behavioral goals. Community members and parents must be asked to join in and become part of the school's leadership team. The role principals' play in advocating outside resources helps build a cooperative and accommodating atmosphere conducive to parental and community involvement in the school.

CHAPTER 4

Role of the Principal: Define Success

In many circumstances, the public school principal's legal authority is set by state law. However, the principal's role in the school system is determined by the school district's superintendent. A principal must lead the school, the teachers, the students, the staff, and the parents who have children enrolled in the school. The vision, purpose, and direction that the school must take to become successful or continue to flourish must be set by the school principal. The school principal must collaborate with all stakeholders in the school to accomplish a set of goals and objectives for students. It is the job of the manager to manage so that the workers and students can see a strong connection between what they are asked to do and what they believe is quality (Glasser, 1992).

School principals must adapt educational behaviors to situations that exist in the school in order to produce positive learning results for their children. Compelling educational administrators display a number of characteristics that distinguish effective styles of leadership from an unsuccessful leadership approach. Intelligence, creativity, inquisitiveness, insight, charisma, and vocal authority are some of the personal attributes and characteristics that distinguish above-average school principals from average school leaders. An effective school principal calculates the best road to take based on the amount of time available to students during the school year. An effective school principal invites others to follow and share in the school's vision.

Principals must remain visible and approachable in order to provide positive direction for students and the staff. Principals must display ingenuity and have the boldness to undertake new ideas and develop positive relations among students, faculty, parents, and the school's community. Effective principals encourage teachers to utilize innovative teaching methods, thereby creating an avenue for professional growth within the school environment. Professional development allows teachers to become facilitators of learning and to share ideas with other educators in the school or school district. Inspired teachers should be able to seek the approval of the principal to include ideas for student learning in the curriculum and the school principal must allow the teacher to initiate the concept after hearing the teacher's proposal. Empowering teachers is one way to initiate change in a school.

Successful school principals continually seek innovative ways to develop every facet of school improvement. Effective principals explore ways to improve schools by changing the status quo when needed, and by giving opportunities to teachers, students, and parents to provide input that can lead to positive school relations. School principals take charge of situations that may have an adverse effect on student learning. They change ineffective school practices swiftly and inform the school staff, students, and parents of new operational procedures in a timely manner. Effective school principals accept responsibility for missteps, address concerns within the school and restore confidence in its system.

Efficient school principals frequently seek ways to make the school more effective by establishing an appropriate climate for student learning. Principals must be perceived as genuine and sincere about making educational achievement and improvement the most important issue in the school, and they must not appear to be going through the motions of running a school. Effective school principals are acutely aware of, understand, and monitor curriculum, instruction, and assessment at all times throughout each school year. A cardinal sin that school principals must avoid is to be blind-sided by curricular, instructional or assessment episodes that happen without their knowledge. It could be quite awkward and embarrassing for the principal to be caught unaware of an incident that happened in the school. How does a public school principal avoid such a discomforting fate?

One technique that may aid principals in eliminating surprises at their schools and help them identify potential pitfalls at the building level entails shrinking the school mentally by taking the roof off and looking into every corner for strengths and weaknesses. Effective school principals keep up to date with what is taking place in all parts of the school and the school boundaries at all times. Utilizing this technique——the school building with its roof removed and the school's boundaries minimized——allows the principal to have a complete picture and an observational tool that decreases the chance of a surprise. The condensed, roofless school method is comparable to clicking a computer's restore-down icon, which reduces the onscreen file and increases the range of vision on the computer screen to allow the user access to more than one image at a time. The technique enables principals to conceptualize how and what is taught to students and it allows the principal a microscopic view of student progress. To keep mentally active, which is essential for principals, requires taking occasional strolls in and around the perimeter of the school, visiting classrooms, talking with teachers and staff, and monitoring lesson plans. Using these techniques allows a hands-on school principal to foresee impending difficulties before being battered with a humiliating scene and ending up in a blind stupor.

Adopting a Philosophy

First-year principals must determine an educational philosophy that defines student success by developing a sound philosophy of learning. The principal's educational philosophy and beliefs will ultimately drive his or her key decisions. They must embody or epitomize the heart and soul of proven methods of student learning. An educational philosophy contains the standards, expectations, principles, and norms that establish the principal's belief system. Although a school principal's educational foundations may evolve from many sources, the belief system should remain grounded in established academic research. What body of evidence does the principal articulate to the school staff that validates and supports his or her philosophical convictions about student learning? School principals must never use unsubstantiated methods for improving academics when dealing with a child's education.

The principal's educational philosophy may be based on many educational theories, however. An educational theory can be as simple as observing the attitudes of students entering and leaving a school bus, or as complex as watching children solve algebraic equations. Successful principals spend time observing students' behavior and watching teachers interact with students and colleagues, as they contemplate conditions in the school that may affect student learning. Observations of the interactions between children and teachers contribute to the formulation of one's philosophy of education. Effective principals make decisions based on observations that affect the student learning process.

An example of this occurs when individual students arrive at school each day. The student focuses his or her vision on the perimeters of the school, scans the grounds and facilities, observes the condition of the school and makes an assumption about the condition, positive or negative, before entering the school. If a student notices that the school yard is unkempt and littered with trash, or the school's property has been defaced to some extent, the student's mind invariably begins to focus on the wretched conditions of the school rather than the learning that is to take place in it that day. To prevent students from focusing on the poor condition of the school's exterior, an effective principal keeps the school grounds well groomed at all times, or in the case of an overnight incident, tries to clean or cover up the unpleasant condition before students arrive. Effective principals take extra steps to eliminate adverse situations that affect student learning. Ineffective principals are not able see that the deplorable conditions at the school affect student learning. Consequently, cleaning up unsightly conditions prior to the students' arrival is not high on their priority list. Reducing the number of depressing or negative sights that surround students at the school helps to eliminate mental barriers to learning. An educator must encourage student learning, not act as a detriment to the student's education.

Treasured School Moments

One school scene repeats itself every year in traditional American schools approximately 230 days after "Auld Lang Syne" rings in a new year. The first letter of the alphabet represents the month that a new school year starts for many children in America and the first letter of the alphabet signals the beginning of the end of the school year. The first letter of the alphabet records and sets the highest criteria and standard for assessing the progress of students in schools.

The first letter of the alphabet epitomizes the mark that all students strive to achieve as learners enrolled in elementary and secondary schools across the country. The first month of a new school year is usually between the end of summer and the beginning of fall. The month signals the time for teachers to report back to school and prepare for students. Each new school year may bring another principal, new teachers and staff to the school. However, each new school year always sees a diverse set of schoolchildren that are different from the preceding school year.

During the summer vacation for teachers and students only a handful of school employees are assigned to schools. In many schools during summer vacation the principal, a secretary or two and a handful of other workers are the only school personnel who remain in the school over the summer months. The school principal will use practically all of each day and week during summer to plan for the new school year. School principals are confronted with a number of school-related issues that must be resolved prior to a new school-year opening. Effective principals know without a doubt that teachers want the school building and its functions to be thoroughly organized, or as near to perfection as possible before they report for the new school year. Missteps by school principals during this holistic planning period could be costly in establishing a smooth school opening and successful school year for students and staff.

A school principal spends most of the summer vacation securing certified and classified staff to fill vacancies. Some school districts provide central office staff to assist in searching for school personnel. On the other hand, in other school districts the school principal must undertake the search, conduct interviews and secure references from former administrators, college professors, and student teacher supervisors. After all the necessary employment documents have been completed, the school principal may recommend candidates' names to the superintendent. The superintendent presents the slate of candidates to the school board for approval. The school board accepts or rejects these candidates at its regularly scheduled school-board meetings throughout the school year. Recommending candidates to the schools superintendent, especially for the important position of classroom teacher, is without a doubt the most important function that a school principal can perform. It is essential that quality classroom teachers are hired and in place on the first day of school. The degree of interaction between teachers and students in the first week of the school year sets the tone and atmosphere for student learning for the remainder of the school year. Information necessary for a successful school year is generated in the initial days of the school year.

Classroom and school rules, regulations, policies, and procedures must be established before teachers can begin their instruction. The first days of school present teachers with the opportunity to capture students' attention by instilling order and discipline and requiring students to develop self-discipline prior to new instruction. Securing the students' attention and keeping them absorbed in their lessons is the key to student learning. Focusing a students' mind on the lesson ensures that student's success during the school year.

Principals are responsible for ensuring that every aspect of the school is sufficiently organized prior to the students' arrival. The school building, empty of teachers and students during summer months, appears as an abandoned community, devoid of the sound of children's laughter, voices, and movement, which characterize school life for ten months of the school year. The school halls and classrooms resonate with silence when teachers and students vacate the school building over the summer months.

Curricular goals are formulated by the school principal, based on the achievement scores of the previous school year and on other data collected during the summer vacation. School climate goals are assessed and devised based on student behavior data accumulated from the preceding year. School principals deal with a number of school-related entities during the summer months. Registering students; assigning duties to staff; organizing departments, teams, and grade levels; planning staff development; completing student, lunch, and bus schedules; revising evacuation plans; completing teacher and student handbooks; organizing textbooks; assigning athletic coaches to duties, if applicable;

assigning student lockers; writing letters to staff, parents, and students; meeting with district leaders, PTA officers, parents, and salesmen; attending workshops; ordering instructional supplies; checking the cleaning progress in classrooms, halls, gymnasiums, cafeteria, and other areas of the building; filling teachers' work requests; checking the landscape and exterior signs; surveying athletic fields; and reviewing and establishing student emergency drills are but a few of the functions the school principal performs and considers before the teachers and students return to school for a new school year.

New School Opening

When schoolteachers report to work for a new school year, the school building becomes converted into a vibrant, charismatic, fast-paced, captivating neighborhood that is alive with happiness. The teachers and assistant teachers (if assigned) scramble around the school receiving and retrieving materials and supplies in anticipation of the students' arrival. The professional work completed by teachers and assistants prior to the students' first week lays the groundwork for meaningful instruction and student learning. Inside the school teachers prepare classroom bulletin boards and decorate the walls so that they will appear interesting and produce positive thoughts in a child's mind.

The first day of school for children in the United States is one of the greatest institutional rituals or traditions that happen in our culture. The opening of a new school year represents togetherness as a society and connects common threads that bond every child and household with school-age children. The excitement builds for parents and students as the new school year approaches. Take a stroll through any commercial establishment that sells school supplies as a new school year approaches and you will see excited students and parents shopping for school items and hoping for a successful school year. The first day of a new school year seizes the hearts of families with schoolchildren, neighborhoods, districts, regions, states, and the nation. The first days of a new school year are sufficiently significant to be covered by print and visual local and national media. That in itself signifies how important the opening of a new school year is to American society.

The opening of a new school year is one aspect of society that unites Americans. Yes, there are other significant grand openings: the opening of a new business, the opening of a professional, collegiate or local schools sports season, opening a new highway or bridge, the opening of an apartment building, a new house, a medical complex, hospital or church. Those openings, however, do not touch the lives of all people in the country and in most cases are more local than national.

The opening of a new school year plays an integral part in the life of every child born in this country and in the lives of school-age children and their families who emigrate to this country. Every child of school age, no matter the race, color, creed, gender, national origin, or primary language, must attend school in this country. What the teacher does on the first day of the new school year shapes the rooms of a child's mind and establishes school principles in all children. The interaction between teachers and students on the first day of school is special and should be boxed up, gift wrapped with a bow and put on a shelf to be preserved as one of the great institutional happenings in American society.

The opening and the closing of a school year is similar to taking a cross-country plane ride. It is always a special time when someone takes a plane ride. There is a sense of anxiety, no matter how many times a person has boarded or exited an airplane. Much like a plane ride, principals and teachers see it as an exciting time of the year, no matter how many times it occurs in their careers.

The empty plane sits at the airport terminal waiting to be filled with passengers much like a school house does during the summer months. An empty school sits on the school grounds waiting to be filled with teachers and children. The captain and his crew enter the plane first, checking to see that the plane is operational and its supplies and features are ready to be used by the passengers. Much like that airplane captain and his crew the principal and his staff enter the school after having first made sure the building and its supplies are ready for the students.

The captain, co-pilot, and crew understand how important each plane trip is to the passengers and how to make the passengers feel as comfortable as possible. Principals, assistant principals, and teachers understand the significance of a new school year, the effect it will have on a child's life, and how important it is to make each student feel special. The passengers walk onto the plane with a ticket in hand that directs them to a specific seat on the plane much like children who arrive on the first day of school with a schedule that directs them to a seat in a classroom.

The plane's crew, seeing new faces for the first time, greets the passengers with a friendly smile and hello. The crew is eager to help the passengers become comfortable much like principals and teachers who greet new students with a smile and a hello and are eager to help students feel at home. The plane's engines roar and it rolls down the runway. As it picks up speed, it shakes and rattles before majestically lifting off the ground and into the air. Similarly, in schools the halls buzz with excitement as children meet and greet teachers and friends, some for the first time, others renewing old acquaintances. Finally, the bell rings, teachers close doors, students focus on teachers, and just like that, the school year is under way.

Along the way the plane stops and refuels. Passengers transfer to connecting flights. Others board the plane, and it takes off again. Similarly, during the school year schools stop for breaks and holidays. Along the way students transfer and new students enroll. Students and staff return from breaks, and school commences again. The plane may experience turbulence as it flies across country toward its final destination. Similarly, a school year may also experience problems.

Finally, the pilot radios the tower for clearance to land and the plane touches down and slowly rolls up to the terminal. Passengers gather their bags and other items and exit the plane. Similarly, a school principal informs parents that the end of the school year is near. On the last days of school, teachers pack books, materials, and supplies for the year and celebrate accomplishments with students. The children snap pictures of friends, hug each other and teachers and share special moments with each other. The final bell rings and the students leave the school building. They walk home or toward buses, cars, and bicycles. Teachers and staff wave to them until the last school bus exits the parking lot. Hopefully, every child had a successful school year. Another year comes to an end. The halls and building echo silence again.

Light the Path: Vision

A great principal has the capacity to be a social architect, one who can change the shape and form of an organization (McCall, 1988). An important duty of a public school principal is to convey to teachers, students, and parents the vision of an exemplary school and the challenges the school may face each year. Effective schools principals insist that the school staff make the vision a reality. Successful principals require the school staff to develop school and student goals that meet reasonable expectations for learning. Public school principals must constantly emphasize and promote the school's vision with students, parents, and the school staff. The principal must be able to show how the mutual interests of the school and its community can be met through commitment to a common purpose. Successful principals look beyond the horizon with enthusiasm and their effective communication skills motivate others to recognize the kind of school that they envision.

Academic areas that need improvement must be addressed rapidly and communicated to students, staff, and parents in a clear, positive, and efficient manner. To develop an effective school the principal provides opportunities for greater teacher and parental input and reinforces the school's vision in all adults who have a stake in the school.

Effective principals have well-defined goals for the school and its staff. Effective principals are willing to bestow upon teachers the latitude to contribute to the attainment of school goals by utilizing their creative talents. The principal authorizes and works earnestly to involve the school's leadership team and its staff in the decision-making process. An effective principal praises staff for the positive work they do and communicates to staff and parents any problems that could be a detriment to a child's success. Successful principals allow teachers to make decisions about student learning through written state and district academic plans. School principals should make teachers feel important and influential by building positive relationships, establishing a mutual trust with them and actively involving them in the planning process. The principal must encourage teachers and staff to take leadership roles in all areas of the school's organization and functions. Some teachers will act on the principal's recommendation while other teachers will abstain from the leadership role. It is important that the principal encourage staff to be leaders. Effective principals present a variety of opportunities for staff members to express their opinions and they take their input into consideration.

The principal must be in tune with all aspects of the school, especially when school district leaders relinquish their control of certain functions. The role played by central office staff to identify needs may vanish in time. To what degree are teachers involved in the decision-making process and to what degree are schools required to be in alignment with the goals and priorities of the school district? At what point are the requests of district leaders for individual school support incorporated into long-term planning for that school? The school principal who has been charged with steering a school toward academic progress must be an advocate for that school.

When the school requests district assistance, the request for help should be expansive, accurate, honest, and justifiable.

Principals must be knowledgeable about the process for seeking help from district leaders. Requesting new capital projects takes time and the principal must provide district leaders with a written detailed summary of the needs of the school. The funding request that the principal prepares for district leaders should be clear and descriptive, and the document must provide substantive information. Principals must keep in mind that other schools in the district also request funding and compete for the same money. The principal should never shortchange teachers and students but must use good judgment when making a funding request. He or she should not overdo the funding request and should avoid the risk of a bad reputation by padding the request. Some school district central office staff oversees funding requests of schools.

Effective principals are able to visualize and prioritize school needs that help the school achieve its stated goals, objectives, and mission. To assist the principal in developing priorities, other high-ranking personnel (high-school department heads, middle-school team leaders, elementary-school grade-level chairpersons, and so forth) should present the principal with a list of needs from the staff's point of view. The list of needs from the staff should cover school items such as instruction and assessment, basic maintenance, safety issues, equipment and supplies that will help teachers advance the academic performance of the students. Items that are mandated by law or must be replaced may require higher priority.

Teachers must be made aware of and understand that it is more difficult to acquire funding for the school staff than it is to obtain funds for children. Prioritizing school needs on emotional feelings or impulse may cause the process to break down, but it is extremely important that all personnel have an avenue to express their opinion in the school-needs process. The creation of a quality school-needs assessment plan necessitates all stakeholders making sound decisions that reflect their mutual interest in the development of schoolchildren.

Principals and teachers should teach character principles in American schools. Schools have the responsibility to teach children the difference between appropriate and inappropriate decisions. Three poignant questions principals should ask and that will help to focus on character standards in public schools are: What are the ideals that I believe in and why do I believe them? How are ethical principles reflected in the school? Are the personal ethics of students, parents, and staff visible in the school? There should be an internal assessment that provides data and insight into behaviors and decisions that differentiate right from wrong for all persons in the school. How will the principal measure the concepts that work well in the school? Teaching character principles should be a cooperative effort between the school and home. Parents must have a thorough understanding of the character principles approved for children by the school or district staff.

Words of a Teacher: What Teachers Say

Principals who consistently praise and acknowledge deserving staff members in written and verbal communications are appreciated. Effective principals recognize and celebrate the achievements of the school staff so that all staff can share the pride of peer accomplishments. Effective principals applaud student and staff achievements and are complimentary of the faculty and staff when they advance student learning.

It would help new and veteran principals to occasionally solicit teachers' opinions on their job performance. The principal's perception of how teachers rate his job performance may be quite different from the teacher's actual assessment. In my second year as a principal, I attended a program that was set up by the state board of education to provide school principals with four weeks of intensive studies on how to become an effective public school principal. Principals from across the state applied for the Principal's Executive Program (PEP) and were required to be approved by the district superintendent prior to selection for a position in the program.

The four weeks of intense instruction were spread out over the course of one school semester. Cohorts of principals attended the program for one week each school month in the semester. The PEP operated much like boot camp for principals and was situated at the University of North Carolina at Chapel Hill. Lodging and most expenses were paid by the state legislature. Principals selected for the program from various school districts from across the state were housed in motels or the university's dormitory. The assignment of dormitory rooms at the university was based primarily on the cost of the program and proximity to the instructional classes. Principals were given numerous educational books and articles and plentiful amounts of assignments to complete and discuss during each instructional session.

One of the first tasks asked principals to survey teachers on their opinion of the principal's performance. The teacher's survey was completely anonymous and was a reversal of the usual evaluation process in that the principal, instead of evaluating teachers, now asked teachers to evaluate his/her performance. It should be a common practice in school districts for teachers to provide input on the principal's performance.

The teachers were asked to select eight characteristics from a list of twenty descriptors that they most closely associated with the principal. Teachers used the program's Inventory of Leadership Practices assessment tool and answered five statements of practices common to effective leaders taken from Jim Kouzes' and

Barry Posner's book, *The Leadership Challenge*. The survey asked the teachers to type their responses and not to use statements that could identify the respondent. At the conclusion of the survey, teachers were told to place the inventory in an envelope, seal the envelope with scotch tape, and give it to the school secretary who would send the collected surveys to the Principal's Executive Program. Each teacher selected to take the survey viewed my job performance at the school differently in their selection of sixteen of twenty characteristics. School principals who were chosen for the program from around the state used the same Inventory of Leadership Practice instrument with their staff.

From the twenty descriptors listed on the inventory instrument the teachers chose the following to characterize my performance. An asterisk denotes that I chose the same characteristics as the teachers to describe my leadership ability: ambitious, broad-minded, caring,* competent,* dependable,* determined, fair-minded, forward-looking, honest,* imaginative, inspiring, intelligent,* mature,* self-controlled,* straight-forward, and supportive were the descriptors chosen by the teachers. There were four characteristics listed on the instrument that were not selected by any of the teachers; cooperative, courageous, independent,* and loyal. One of the four traits that was not chosen by the teachers, independent, was favored by the principal.

The survey information received from the teachers was shared with the principals at the first PEP weekly session. The result of the teachers' surveys was shared with the staff upon my return to the school in a faculty meeting with teachers and staff. The information derived from the surveys provided valuable insight for me because the feedback came from the people who matter the most in the school: the teachers. As a young principal, knowing that the teachers were supportive of my efforts to lead them boosted my confidence that the school was headed in the right direction. The Principal Executive Program sessions that were set up by the state board of education served their purpose because the program made me more insightful as a young public school principal. The principal sessions set by the state board and legislature may have served an additional purpose in that when the principal was away the functional operations of the school were entrusted to the assistant principal. This allowed the assistant principal to grow into the role of administrator by making decisions affecting the school, its teachers, and students.

CHAPTER **5**

The Role of Teachers

In the effective school, the principal acts as an instructional leader and effectively and persistently communicates the mission to staff, parents, and students (Lezotte, 2004). Although it has been documented that the principal should lead the instructional program in the school, it is the presence of quality classroom teachers that is the single most determining factor in helping children to learn. The teachers' role in the learning process requires that they close the students' external mental door. It is the door in the room of the mind that students like to open because it leads to the outside world during lessons. Closing a child's external mental door during the lesson is by far the toughest chore a teacher must perform in the classroom. Closing a child's external door means that the teacher has captured the full attention of the student during instruction. The external door should only be opened during instruction to allow the student to retrieve information experienced externally.

A classroom teacher must exhaust all possible means to keep the external door closed during instructional time. The ability of a teacher to seize and maintain the attention of a student during instruction is the major attribute that separates the best teachers from marginal teachers. The teacher's ability to focus students on the lesson does not constitute command of the students' minds. However, it controls the flow of information in the classroom by limiting the number of times a student can venture into the outside world, which will eventually interfere with student's learning. Teachers are labeled ineffective because of their inability to close the mental door that so many students like to open during the instructional time. The failure of a teacher to capture a child's attention during class time resides in the fact that ineffective teachers do not use substantive activities, ideas, responses, and examples to capture a student's attention. Effective teachers have the ability to close the student's external mental door during learning time because they make learning clear-cut and unpretentious.

The main goal of a classroom teacher is to control the number of times students are allowed to exit the room of learning to retrieve information that links them to what is being taught. The teacher should allow students to go to the outside world only for a brief moment or seconds to retrieve information needed for the lesson, after which they should immediately close the outside door and usher the students back into the room of learning. Effective teachers are well prepared and adept at presenting relevant examples and information that allow students to find something in their lives that connects them to the lesson.

Who is better at charting a curriculum course than those at the helm? Public school principals should have firsthand knowledge of curricula and instruction, but it is the classroom teacher who nurtures a child until the brain blossoms in the learning process. Schools governed by principals who were perceived by their teachers to be strong instructional leaders exhibited significantly higher scores in reading and mathematics than did schools operated by average and weak instructional leaders (Smith and Andrews, 1989).

What Children Know: How Parents Find Out

Public school principals are responsible for overseeing the instructional and managerial programs of the schools that they are appointed to lead. Schoolteachers and principals must understand the intricacies of the content to be taught and how the instructional process works. Parents should receive substantial information about the school from their children during the school year. Over the course of a school year parents frequently ask their children what they learned from their teachers rather than what the principal said to their children. Parents want to know what the teacher taught the child that enhanced the child's knowledge. Most children do not know what the principal does at school from one day to the next. Children are simply more in tune with their teachers than they are with the school principal. Teachers also see relatively little of the principal during a school day. Their close interaction with schoolchildren give them most of the responsibility for ensuring that schoolchildren are able to grasp the content of each subject taught.

Children very seldom talk about the school principal with their parents. They talk more about their teachers. They may discuss with their parents information communicated to the student body by the principal, announcements heard over the public address system, or announcements made by school staff and approved by the principal. However, unless the information that the principal communicates to students is of importance to them, it may not be shared directly with parents. School principals disseminate information to students using the school's public address system, through school assemblies, in handouts delivered to parents, or by other means. The information may or may not reach parents if it is left up to the child to deliver it.

School principals usually talk to parents at PTA meetings and planned parent activities, through newsletters, at open house, through telephone calls, web page contact and through other school activities and materials. Children's teachers should communicate with parents more often than the school principal. Parents may not know their children's school principal as well as they know their children's teachers. Parents generally know who the principal is but often do not personally know the principal as they do their children's teachers. Therefore, many parents will seek conferences with their children's teachers or ask to speak with the assistant principal before requesting to have a conference with the school principal.

The same phenomenon occurs in other walks of life including business, the military, law enforcement, sports teams, media, and so forth. Most employees will talk first with the plant's foreman instead of taking their concerns to the plant manager. A professional athlete will talk first with the team's head coach or general manager before knocking on the team owner's door. In cases where grade-level assistant principals work directly with parents, it is very common for parents to ask for a conference with the assistant principal rather than the principal because parents have probably forged a relationship with the assistant principal rather than with the principal.

Disconnected Learning: Parental Inquiry

It has always been a prime responsibility of parents to balance the serious matters that their children need to learn with the distractions of entertainment and play (Bennett, 1986). Concerned parents who see problems with how and what their child is learning in school will exhaust all conferences with their child's teacher or assistant principal before requesting a conference with the school principal. During such a conference the school principal must exercise his/her knowledge of the course content information being discussed, the written curriculum, and teacher methodology and articulate what the school system expects of the child in the learning process. The principal must explain how children are taught in public school, discuss research that explains how children learn, and give parents a broad overview of educational theory and practice.

The principal must share with parents how learning one subject's information may impact teaching another subject that the child may take in the future. Parents will rely on the school principal to be the ultimate authority on student learning and knowledgeable about subject matter. Otherwise, if given a choice, they will bypass the principal's office to talk with someone else in the school system that can help them. A conference with the school principal may be the first time that a parent speaks directly with the school principal. Therefore, when a parent requests a conference, the principal must prepare for it by reviewing all available information and documentation.

Principals must be able to assure the parent that they know the parent child academic standing. Parents want to know that the principal entrusted with their child five days of the week cares deeply for their child. Before the conference, in addition to reviewing documentation concerning the child, the principal should speak to the child's teachers, guidance counselor(s), assistant principal(s), and other school personnel to obtain information that will help him or her to make an informed decision. All individuals with pertinent information may have to be placed on standby if the principal needs more information on the day of the conference.

Parents not only know their child's teachers but try to form cordial relationships with them because they view them as having the most impact on their child's ability to learn. The principal's role in school conferences is to arrange requested parental visits or provide opportunities for parents to discuss their concerns with the teacher(s) or other school personnel. The principal leads the instructional process at school, but the teacher delivers what is required for students to learn. While instructional leadership remains important, the concept has broadened. Leadership is viewed as broadly to include all adults, especially teachers (Lezotte, 2004). A first-rate classroom teacher is far more important to the child's learning process than the school principal, superintendent, or school board members.

Teachers formulate opinions on the character principles that are important for a student to succeed. They are based in part on the teacher's past experiences as a student. Teachers choose what they consider to be first-rate character principles and decide how excellence is to be measured and achieved. Many school districts have incorporated character principles into the curriculum. Teachers have tremendous latitude in working with children in classrooms and in determining the purpose of and how to pursue education. Teachers are the most powerful people in a school and as a group, the most potent unit in the school district because of the influence they have on children. When teachers make decisions on what to teach children their assessment should be based on the gains or losses that students incur during the learning process. Effective classroom teachers recognize that the success of a child is dependent upon making adjustments in lessons at all times during the instructional period, especially after the teacher has analyzed student performance and data.

First-Year Teacher Experience

In a teacher's first year, the teacher must make constant modifications to become an expert on the curriculum, adjust delivery of effective and meaningful instruction and understand how the assessment of the child is connected to the overall teaching and learning process. Time and again teachers think they are teaching the content well, but in reality they are not. First-year teachers need constant monitoring and immediate feedback on teaching practices, whether it is positive or negative, in order to improve aspects of their instruction and their management of the classroom. In their first year of teaching teachers will undergo adjustments to matters such as educational beliefs and philosophies, how to communicate with children, and the best way to deliver instruction before they become efficient deliverers of instruction. Madeline

Hunter defined teaching as a constant stream of professional decisions made before, during, and after interaction with the students. Such decisions are implemented to increase the probability of learning, (Gentile, 1988).

When I entered the teaching profession, one important aspect of teaching that I thought about the most was the need to evaluate myself day to day, week to week and month to month. Since first-year teachers are dependent upon veteran teachers for help, I wanted to absorb all the knowledge I could about teaching children so that I could become an independent teacher almost immediately. What did others, especially the students, think of my performance as a new teacher? Were the concepts that I taught to students working? If so, how would I know that the concepts were working? What could I do as a first-year teacher to make classroom presentations better for students? What could I do too rally my students so that they could learn at their peak proficiency rate? How could I get the students more engaged in the learning process? What priorities must be established in teaching and learning to ensure that the students would have academic success? Those were some of the questions that I pondered over and over in my mind and shared with my colleagues from the first day that I stepped into a classroom. Soon into the first year I realized that it was my responsibility to help my students advance by providing them excellent instruction for the duration of time that they were to be with me.

First-year teachers must understand that they are not entirely responsible for laying a child's entire educational foundation. It takes many teachers working many years to complete the education of a child. Building a child's education over the years is much like building a new house. Getting started on a new house involves planning, permits, and inspections. Similarly, in pre-school there are plans, lesson themes, and inoculations to complete. Building a new house involves foundations, plumbing, heating, electrical and water hookups. Similarly, in kindergarten the basic education involves reading, writing, spatial sense, visual arts, music, numbers, numbers sense, and an introduction to science. Building a new house involves framing the house and adding the roof, doors, and windows. In elementary school the major features of study——language arts, mathematics, social studies, science, the arts, and physical activities——make up a child's education.

Much like the inspections that are required to measure progress as the house is constructed; teacher-made tests, standardized assessment, progress reports, and report cards sent home to parents' measure a student's progress during the school year. At the midway point construction the house goes through many visual changes, especially in the exterior and flooring, including brick work, siding, gutters, driveway, decking, garage doors and landscaping. It is like middle school where the students pass through the critical point of schooling in their life. The change from childhood to adolescence is a tremendously important time. As they move through middle school, children undergo physical, mental, and social changes.

The last phase in building a house involves completing the interior of the house: adding the dry wall, insulation, cabinets, light fixtures, tiles, carpet or hardwood floors, and painting the interior. The last phase of a students' education involves completing high school. High schools are diverse institutions with architectural and structural features that are vastly different than elementary and middle schools. The students' intellectual capacity is greatly challenged. They experience vast differences in aspirations, interests, and values. High-school students have an infinite range of physiological differences. The newly built house undergoes a final inspection before a family moves into it. Seniors take final examinations prior to moving out of high school and into society as well-educated individuals. Preschool teachers, elementary-school teachers, middle-school teachers and high-school teachers should take pride in the part they play in shaping the students who make the journey through the school system into well-rounded individuals.

Effective teachers are relentless at seeking the success of each child they teach and eventually take the position that no matter what a student's background may be, a way can be found to help that student succeed in school. An effective teacher searches for the positive aspects of a child's life to help that child. The search could involve looking at the child's cognitive domain, the affective domain, or psychomotor domains to induce the student to learn. Effective teachers know that there are other aspects of the child's life that may be improved socially, emotionally, physically, or intellectually.

Much of a teacher's first year concerns what the teacher does not know about the mechanics of teaching. First-year teachers must constantly evaluate their performance. They must connect the theories and methodologies of teaching learned prior to entering the teaching field and merge them with practice. Except for limited training at the collegiate level, first-year teachers undertake tasks that they have never been involved with before. The duties performed by first-year teachers place them at the autonomous stage on Abraham Maslow's pyramid. The first-year teacher who reached self-actualization as a college student is likely to regress from self-actualization to autonomy before moving back to self-actualization when they become quality teachers. When a first-year teacher moves from college life to the classroom the change is likely to cause a paradigm shift. At this point they need support and encourage from the principal, mentor teacher, and other competent qualified leaders in the school and school district. First-year teachers should take advantage of down time in the school calendar——school workdays or holidays——to assess their performance in the classroom.

What to Look for in a First-Year Teacher

As a principal I evaluated teachers on how they performed in and outside the classroom in their first year. However, it was during the teachers' second year that their performance was evaluated most critically. An ineffective principal can shove a potentially good teacher away from the teaching profession by reacting as if that teacher should be experienced enough to exhibit perfection in the classroom. An ineffective first-year teacher and poorly experienced teachers blame academic failure on the child's inability to learn rather than on their own lack of teaching ability. Ineffective teachers view their ability to teach children as well above average and their students' ability to learn as well below average.

It is not what the teacher does in the first year. Rather, it is how the teacher performs in the classroom as a second-year teacher that counts the most, provided the teacher shows some ability to engage students in the first year. Most teachers would admit that first-year teaching is a difficult task. Many of us also need to admit, sheepishly, that our teaching improves in subsequent years because we can use seniority to our benefit by creating a better teaching situation (Glickman, Gordon, Ross-Glickman, 1995). If teachers do not possess the cognitive ability to assess, evaluate, and make changes to their teaching between the first and second year, more than likely they will remain at the same level throughout their teaching career. I believe the greatest time for change occurs between the first and second year of teaching, considering that first-year teachers need sufficient time to digest the demands of teaching. They must have time to adjustment to the teaching process.

If the teacher exhibits poor teaching ability in the second year as well as in the first year, then divine intervention must take place between him or her, the principal, and district leaders. If the teacher does not change weak teaching behaviors between year one and year two and continues to teach children, that teacher will eventually be responsible for shortchanging the education of hundreds, maybe thousands, of children during his or her career, and that would be totally unacceptable. Effective principals are astute enough to recognize when new teachers are headed in the wrong direction and they take steps to redirect them.

Teachers are knowledgeable about what content should be included and taught in the curriculum. They make decisions about scope and sequence, and they can be consultants to other teachers if they are trained to gather and assimilate data correctly. They are expected to break down volumes of educational content into understandable, relevant information that zeros in on a student's weaknesses and strengths. Effective teachers encourage and motivate students by recognizing their accomplishments and finding suitable opportunities to celebrate student achievements. Effective teachers let students know that the positive efforts that they exhibit in class are special and truly appreciated.

CHAPTER 6

Role of Students: Breadth of Knowledge

Human beings are endowed with an exceptional gift——the brain——an internal body organ and the center of intelligence, understanding, and common sense that allows an individual the mental power to think and reason. The brain separates human beings from the animal kingdom. Several elaborate systems of learning lie within the brain. According to the American College of Physicians complete Home Medical guide (Goldmann and Horowitz, 2003), the cerebral cortex governs higher brain functions, including thought. The cerebral cortex receives and processes sensations, regulates senses of the body, and makes language possible. Unlike the animal kingdom, the brain allows humans the ability to think, reason, and probe complex processes. Information observed by the eyes, for instance, travels instantaneously to the cerebral cortex for clarity and comprehension. Words lifted by the eyes from reading materials, or heard through the ears, advances expeditiously to the cerebral cortex for logical and clear understanding.

Human thoughts occur in milliseconds. However, the mind pays conscious attention to one train of thought at a time. What influences individuals to pay attention to their thought processes? What motivates individuals to grasp knowledge during the learning process? Learning is an activity of the brain, under the direct control of the individual and most of the time results in additions or modifications to the individual's memory. Anything less is not learning. The responsibility for engaging in learning belongs to the individual. Learning is not automatic. Rather, it requires a sustained and conscious effort on the part of the individual (Letteri, 1985). The ability of a teacher to capture the attention of a student during a classroom learning activity is the key to teaching. The teacher's responsibility is to redirect the child's occupied mind toward the lesson because learning is an activity of the brain under the direct control of the individual. The two lower systems of the brain, the brain stem and limbic system, strongly influence what students pay attention to and find important.

Letteri reasons that new and old information must link together. Without the linkage, new information may be lost to memory and the task to be completed by the student will not be undertaken successfully. Materials and information delivered to students must be meaningful and relevant. John Dewey stated that to know mind, as distinct from mental qualities, one has to address things that are not mind or mental and translate the phenomena that immediately occur into a set of connections between events.

The student's brain, when placed in stressful conditions such as disorder in the classroom, creates closure of the neocortex, which reverts back to the lower levels. Regression to the lower levels of the brain results in decreased rational and creative thought. It becomes extremely difficult for the student to pay attention to the teacher. A nonthreatening environment is essential for the neocortex to operate at peak efficiency so that the brain can allow meaningful learning to take place. It is vitally important for classroom teachers to capture their students' attention and maintain order and discipline within the class the moment students enter the classroom.

The human brain, which has been studied for centuries, permits a person's mind to wander endlessly through internal and external images or processes. A person's mental aptitude ranges from conscious thought to daydreaming and introspective thinking. The human mind has the ability to transcend space and time.

It is multifaceted and made up of many folds associated with internal processes in the brain including imagination, consciousness, beliefs, willpower, intellect, personality, and the ability to make reasoned and rational choices.

John Dewey (1966) stated that it is evident that certain doctrines about the nature of the mental allow only for introspection. Dewey equated introspection with an immediate or intuitive act by an individual. An individual's mental range, scope, dimension, measure, mental expansion, vision, or broadmindedness is what allows the brain's mind to increase or home in on a precise thought. The human brain's mental capacity has the ability to expand as far as an individual chooses, or can be limited to a single task or thought.

Individual Quadrants for Success Model

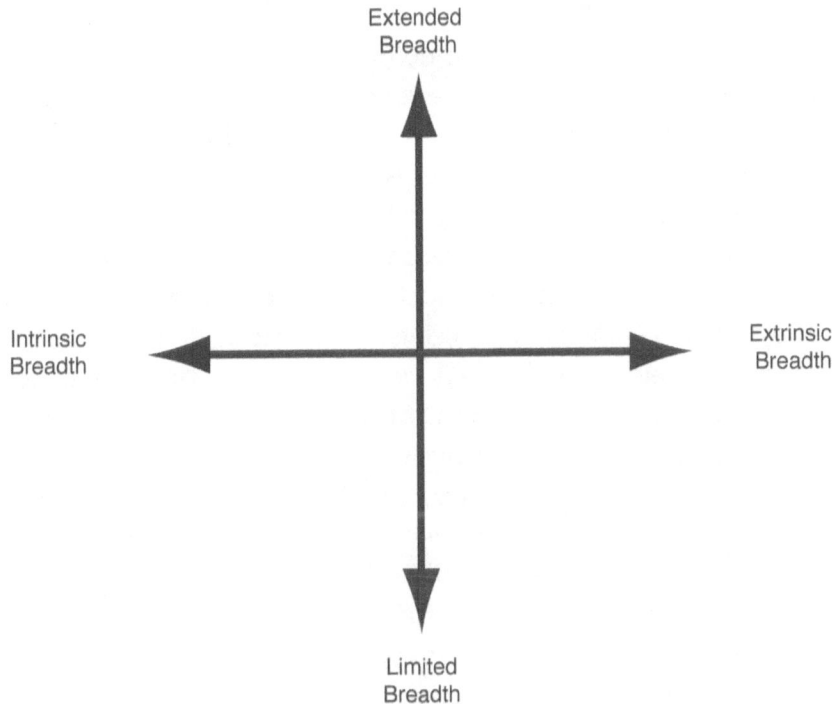

Extended
Breadth

Intrinsic
Breadth

Extrinsic
Breadth

Limited
Breadth

The good news is that the more we discover about how the brain learns, the more successful teaching and learning can be. The bad news is that we cannot get this information to teachers fast enough (Sousa, 1995).

The Individual Quadrants for Success Model (IQSM) divides the brain into four quadrants. In the graphic model they are separated equally by intersecting horizontal and vertical lines. One half of the brain contains intrinsic breadth mental stimuli and the other half of the brain contains extrinsic breadth mental stimuli. Intrinsic breadth is located on the left side of the quadrants and shares similarities with the left brain functions of analysis, logic, and sequential thinking. The right side of the model, extrinsic breadth, reflects right-brain qualities that focus on visuals.

The Individual Quadrants for Success Model envisions four rooms of the mind that harness a person's thoughts and actions. The rooms of the mind are located at the center of the brain where information is received from the teacher that is critical to student learning. In many instances learning is driven by an individual's perception of the environment or is self-imposed by external and internal means. The ability to pay attention and focus on the task at hand is the key element in the learning process when the doors to the individual quadrants are unlocked and opened. Humans in all walks of life——educators, business, politicians, attorneys, doctors, military personnel, bankers, white collar workers, blue collar workers, the retired population, all working sectors, young and old, rich and poor——consciously move in and out of the rooms of the mind each second of every minute of the hour. Information, relevant and irrelevant, is received, processed and analyzed continuously throughout the four rooms of the model.

The Individual Quadrants for Success Model entails establishing goals that are controlled by the student or regulated by the teacher and extend to out-of-class activities. These include organizing tasks that may or may not be completed by the student prior to embarking upon other goals or tasks. It is also important that the teacher occupy the student with out-of-classroom activities. It has been reported that the amount of homework that students are engaged in each day has a bearing on academic achievement. A National Commission on Time and Learning study (1993) revealed that assigning, grading, or commenting on homework had three times as much effect on achievement as a child's family's economic status. The commission reported that in the United States, Japan, and China, the amount of time students spend studying after school is significantly related to improvement in math and reading scores. However, academic achievement declined in the three countries as students became more engaged in nonacademic activities such as working, watching television, or being with friends.

The commission's analysis discovered that only 6 percent of nine-year-old students completed two or more hours of homework each day in American schools. In contrast, the percentage of students in ten developed countries who engaged in two or more hours of homework per day ranged from 13 to 35 percent. In a comparison of thirteen-year-old students, 29 percent of students in the United States completed two or more hours of homework each day, but in fifteen countries abroad, the average number of students who completed two or more hours of homework daily was 45 percent.

Extended breadth is located at the top of the vertical line in the Individual Quadrant for Success Model. Extended breadth allows an individual to extend and expand his or her mental capacities infinitely. Extended breadth stretches an individual's mental capacity to its farthest breadth and depth. The range of a person's mental power is limitless and vast. Extended breadth is like receiving a gift from a loved one, slowly pulling the ribbons from the package and removing the specially designed gift-wrap to open the package. The person receiving the gift stares at the wrapped package and all of its beauty and splendor, but it is what is inside the package that creates the expectancy. The mind wonders endlessly, contemplating what could be inside an exceptional and beautifully decorated gift box. Anticipating the item inside the box brings love and pleasure to the giver and the receiver. It is like opening a window shade or pulling the curtains back each morning and looking outside to view what Mother Nature has to offer for the day. The view of the sky each day is never the same, just as there is always knowledge to be attained. Extended breadth allows an individual to expand the mind and accept and process external stimuli and images that enhance the student's thinking.

Each student's extended breadth is unique to that student, just as individuals have unique finger prints and daydreams. How images are processed in the mind differs from one individual to another. Two individuals cannot perceive visual images in exactly the same way even when the images are visible to both individuals and their descriptions of the images may be very similar. Although we share physical features that receive stimuli, we are all unique in our interpretation of the information and in the manner in which we use such information to construct reality (Nalour, 1985).

The bottom of the vertical line of the Individual Quadrant for Success Model is limited breadth. Limited breadth narrows an individual's mental scope to concentrate on a single task or tasks. It closes a person's mind to distracting external images or internal stimuli.

A task is concrete and based in reality requiring time and space to complete. Limited breadth requires total focus on a task. It is manifested on a person's face in a look of total concentration. The eyes may be set deep in the socket and squint to allow the individual to focus more intently on the task at hand. Deep focus produces an unmistakable, physical characteristic. The famous New York Yankees baseball catcher, Yogi Berra, once said, "You can't think and hit at the same time." Yogi Berra was correct in that the completion of a task requires internal focus. The mind must be cleared of external stimuli to allow concentration on the particular task at hand. It is virtually impossible for a batter to hit the ball if he is thinking about something other than making contact with the ball.

A CAT scan of a professional golfer's brain activity and a scan of a casual golfer's brain activity taken at the point of striking the ball showed vast differences between the professional golfer and the casual golfer. The casual golfer's brain scan showed a tremendous amount of activity in the brain at the moment when he made contact with the ball, whereas there was virtually no activity in the professional golfers' brain at the moment of contact. The professional golfer was able to clear his mind of all external and internal stimuli and concentrate totally on striking the golf ball.

The casual golfer, on the other hand, had difficulty clearing his mind of internal or external thoughts prior to striking the ball. He was therefore more erratic in striking the golf ball. The fact that differences in brain activity existed between the casual and professional golfer suggests that the disparity between the quality of the novice golfer's performance and the expert golfer's performance can be traced to the level of organization of neural networks during motor planning. In particular, extensive practice over a long period of time leads experts to develop a focused and efficient organization of task-related neural networks, whereas novices have difficulty filtering out irrelevant information (Milton, Solodkin, Hlustik, & Small, 2007).

There are times when someone may concentrate on a specific task oblivious to his surroundings. An example of limited breadth occurs when a person decides to watch a television show. As he enters the room his eyes may focus on several objects located throughout the room including other people who may be in the room. After visually exploring the interior features of the room, the viewer diverts his attention from the objects in the room and redirects his attention to the visual images emanating from the television. At some point the other objects in the room become nonexistent to his conscious mind. The other objects in the room, which may include another person or persons in close proximity, are completely removed from the viewer's consciousness. At that point the viewer's mind becomes completely fixated on a single task: concentration on the images coming from the television screen.

If, while watching the television show, the viewer's attention is broken, all of the objects and persons in the room become visible again. The viewer's attention may be broken by another person entering the room, by commercial breaks in the program, or by other attention-breaking phenomena. The voice of another person in the room, the sound of a vehicle's motor, a horn blowing from a vehicle as it passes by on the street, the sound of a barking dog, or the rings from a telephone may interrupt the viewer's focus. Breaks in concentration may last for several seconds or minutes, but eventually the viewer will return to the task of concentrating on the program.

On the left side of the horizontal line is intrinsic breadth. Intrinsic breadth is the ability to exist comfortably within one's own mental makeup. Intrinsic breadth is grounded in the principle of introversion in that it addresses the ability to be insightful and reflective. The left side of the brain deals with logic, words, parts, specifics, analysis, and sequential thinking. Intrinsic breadth is time bound in that there is a sense of time, goals to be completed, and the individual's relationship to those goals.

Intrinsic breadth is closely associated with a person's affective domain; it is associated with emotions. Intrinsic breadth is a person's point of view, outlook, stance, position, opinion, way of thinking, or intuitive hunch. Intrinsic breadth is an individual's ability to sit quietly with the body still and eyes closed and prevent the mind from thinking about anything. It is the ability to conduct a self-assessment or analyze inner strengths and weaknesses. The degree to which individuals are successful in life depends largely on their knowing what they do well. Their strong suits, assets, power, talents, positive features, and the advantages they believe they have in life are their ace in the hole. Successful individuals possess the ability to continuously evaluate their limitations. If a male student recognizes that he is a poor speller, he can mitigate that weakness by having his work proofed by someone who spells well. He can use a dictionary and the spelling checker on the word processor before printing the final document for his teacher.

Important as it is for students to learn the basics of reading, writing, and mathematics, it is equally important that they know themselves, internalize their strengths and weaknesses and understand how they are perceived by others. Students' success comes as a result of their familiarity with their strengths and weaknesses. Individuals should be able to achieve success or acquire what they need in life to be successful through initiative, willpower, and their own resourceful endeavors.

Located on the right side of the horizontal line is extrinsic breadth. Extrinsic breadth encompasses all of the external stimuli present in the life of an individual. Extrinsic breadth encompasses the exterior mental imagery of the individual. It is the totality of all facets of sight, everything that an individual can see or visualize through the senses. It includes listening to a recorded message or reading a passage from a book. It consists of the observable and the concealed, obvious and hidden mental capacities. It is overt and covert. It may apply directly to the individual's learning process or it may not have any bearing on the individual's learning.

The right quadrants are linked to external images. They embrace the whole picture and relationships among parts, synthesis, and simultaneous and holistic thinking. The right side of the brain is time free in that it may lose a sense of time altogether.

Extrinsic Extended Breadth Quadrant: The Exterior Room

When individuals extend their breadth of knowledge extrinsically or externally they become aware of events taking place in their external life. Extrinsic extended breadth refers to stimuli that occur outside a person's mind. It is the mental quadrant that, when opened, provides a pathway that leads to the student's outside world. More than any of the other quadrants of the model the extrinsic extended breadth quadrant is the greatest detriment to student learning during instructional time. Some environmental circumstances and external stimuli cannot be controlled by the student. Inescapable external mental images occur daily in students' lives and may have a profound effect on how they learn. Each day before they leave home for school, children are influenced by events in their lives. The family lifestyle, listening to the radio, or watching television play a part in a child's life outside school. When a student walks to the bus stop, he observes the neighborhood and studies the changes in the outside world.

When students ride a school bus, a car, a bicycle, or walk to school, they are confronted by interpersonal and intrapersonal circumstances. The teacher may never know if an unusual event occurred in the neighborhood or if the student had an unusual experience while traveling to school. Did a strange mental image enter the brain of the child before leaving home for school, or while riding or walking to school? Did the child see something that became planted in his mind on the way to school and that may affect his ability to learn? Did he witness an accident involving other vehicles or a school bus? Was the child's mind full of images and sounds of emergency vehicles, police cars, flashing lights, blasting sirens, an injured person, or crowds gathered around an accident scene?

The child, not the teacher, knows what type of climate prevails at home, in the neighborhood, or on the school bus. Even after the child arrives at school, he may be confronted with an unusual event before he meets with his teachers. Did the student have a normal or abnormal start to the school day? Many remote events occur over the course of the school day, which may affect the learning process. Bearing this in mind, administrators and teachers must work vigorously to limit the amount of extraneous exterior images and information that filters into a child's mind before learning takes place.

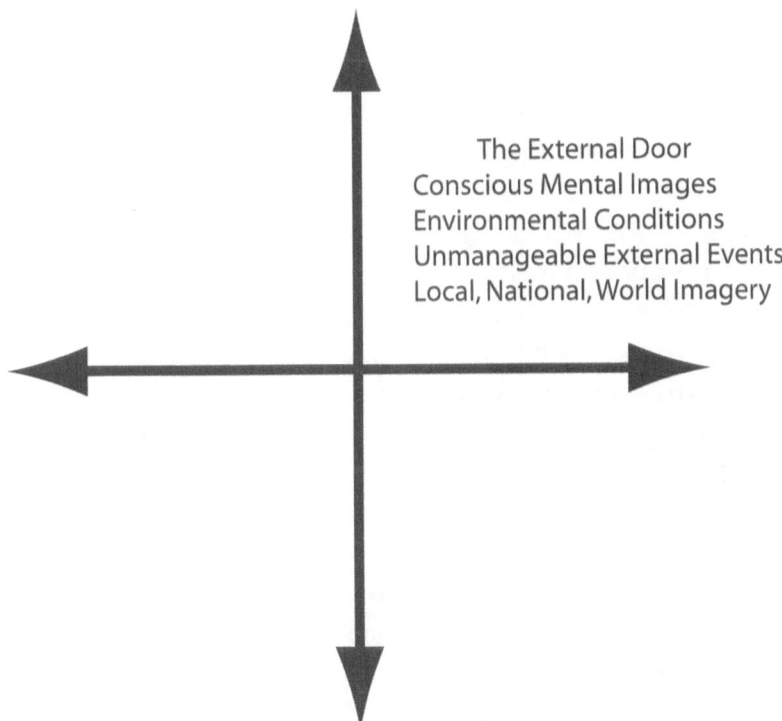

The External Door
Conscious Mental Images
Environmental Conditions
Unmanageable External Events
Local, National, World Imagery

Verbal and visual external events on local, national, and worldwide levels frequently enter a child's mind. Each generation of schoolchildren witnesses unforeseen events throughout their school years. How do such incidents impact the child's learning process? Is there any effect at all? The high-school seniors whom I taught in my first year as a teacher in 1977 grew up in turbulent times. The seventeen-year-old seniors were born in 1960, near the end of the baby-boomer cycle. Baby boomers are generally considered to have been born between 1946 and 1964. Those high-school seniors entered kindergarten in 1965, middle school in 1971, and high school in 1974. They witnessed affirmative action and the Vietnam War, which divided the nation. They observed four college students protesting the Vietnam War being gunned down by National Guardsmen at Kent State University in Ohio.

The high-school seniors whom I taught grew up when college students were shot down on a college campus even as many of them were preparing to enter college themselves. Eyewitness accounts informed them of the forced entry into the Democratic Party headquarters, the Watergate scandal, and the resignation of the American president, Richard Nixon. They learned that for the first time in history a sitting U.S. president had to leave office in disgrace. As part of their American history or civic lessons, schoolchildren are taught about presidents who are elected to serve the highest office in the nation. All students are taught that the office of U.S. president is the most powerful in the nation and the free world. What happens in a child's mind when there is a scandal surrounding the president of the United States? Does it affect the child in a classroom setting? The seniors in my first year of teaching lived in the era when the United States Supreme Court legalized abortion in Roe v. Wade. Those seniors grew up when black students were bused into white neighborhood schools and white students were bused into black neighborhood schools because the Supreme Court of the United States ruled that forced busing was nationally lawful. The seniors saw legislation P.L 94-142 establish education for all handicapped children.

Students grow up in times when national events take a toll on families, adults, and children. The first-year senior students whom I taught were not indifferent by any stretch of the imagination; they appeared restless and defiant. What I learned very early as a first-year teacher was that the problem was not with the students; the problem lay with me. I learned that it was my responsibility to close the students' extrinsic extended breadth quadrant and bring them into the room of learning. To expect the children to be perfect angels, to be obedient and orderly was a grave mistake. To assume that all the schoolchildren would conduct themselves appropriately in the classroom was my mistake. It is a mistake that all first-year teachers must overcome if they are to lead school-children to success.

A beginning high-school teacher in 2007 taught senior students born in 1990. The seniors in 2007 started kindergarten in 1995, middle school in 2001, and high school in 2004, assuming they were successful at each grade level. When those seniors entered kindergarten they were confronted with daily television news accounts of a well-known professional football player who was on trial for killing his ex-wife and her companion. The trial and its verdict would plunge a dagger into the hearts and minds of our citizens. The trial divided the nation racially. The senior students of 2007 heard accounts of a U.S. veteran who bombed a federal building in Oklahoma City. By the time they were in third grade two high-school students would open fire and kill fourteen students and one teacher and wound twenty-three others at Columbine High School in Littleton, Colorado. The massacre would change safety procedures in schools across America.

Entering middle school, these students would witness another presidential scandal in the White House. President Bill Clinton was impeached for sexual misconduct. Another president, George W. Bush, entered the White House under a cloud of suspicion after an election flawed by malfunctioning voting booths in the state of Florida. In the seniors' first year in middle school, nineteen foreign terrorists hijacked airplanes bound for U.S. cities and successfully crashed two of them into the World Trade Center in New York City's financial district. A third plane crashed into the Pentagon in Washington D.C. while apparently headed for the White House, and a fourth plane crashed before hitting its target, an unspecified national treasure.

The seniors witnessed the United States declaration of war on Afghanistan and Iraq and saw the first state in the union allow same-sex marriages. By their sophomore year in high school these students had seen a natural disaster, Hurricane Katrina, destroy much of the Gulf Coast and parts of the city of New Orleans,

Louisiana. They were exposed to the pain of human suffering that followed that event.

It is difficult to determine the mental effect major events have on children's minds as they move through the educational system. Educators, especially teachers and administrators, should assume that major events to which children are exposed have some influence on their social, emotional, or psychological state of mind as they move from early childhood through the adolescent years. For it is during children's early years in school that they begin to form opinions of the events and issues that will shape their adult life. When an intense external event takes place in a child's life, the child does not have time to stop and think of the implications. Teachers and school administrators play an important role in keeping students calm and engaged in the learning process during troubling times. When emotional events affect children in the learning environment the decisions made by the principal and teachers determine learning outcomes. The school principal must lead the school, its staff, and children during emotionally stressful times.

The morning of September 11, 2001 started out as another normal school day for teachers and students of the middle school where I was principal. It was school as usual that early September morning until a sixth-grade language arts teacher ran to my office and informed me that one of the twin towers was on fire in New York City. Having worked as a college student during one summer vacation in that part of the city, I knew the area well and because my sister worked in the twin towers, I needed more information about the situation. As I watched the events unfold that bright, sunny day, I became mesmerized in disbelief at the events unfolding on the television in the school's media center.

The school's media coordinator and I were the only people watching the event in the media center. I watched as the news reports stated the probable cause for the incredible fire and black smoke that spewed out from one of the towers. I watched as the news channel cut from the incident at the tower to show the president of the United States, George W. Bush, at the moment when he was informed of the plane strikes on the twin towers. The image of the president speaking to a group of elementary students was vivid and striking. I watched in astonishment as the second tower was hit by plane number two and smoke and ashes blew across the city's skyline. Thoughts ran through my mind as, horrified, I watched one of the city's great landmarks burn.

The city of New York without a doubt is one of the country's shining stars, a place that everyone in and outside America dreams of visiting. I watched as the first of the two megastructures tumbled to earth like a set of crashing dominoes, one floor after another. It was the moment when the first tower, pierced by a plane, disappeared from the city's skyline that determined whether I would address the situation with students and staff. Should the day's instructional procedures be interrupted to deliver a message concerning the World Trade Center? News of an event of that magnitude would travel fast throughout the school whether or not I spoke to the school.

Unless proper instructions were delivered to the teachers and students on how to proceed for the remainder of the school day, the educational goals for the school day would quite possibly be lost entirely. I left the media center knowing that the twin-tower event would cause tremendous grief and emotion for the teachers and children at the school. According to the media reports there were deaths and the staff and students could have had family members working in the towers just as I had a sister who worked in one of them.

In my sixteen years as a principal, I've had to make decisions involving events many times. It comes with the territory but never grows old. Principals and teachers must do everything within their power to preserve the teaching and learning environment by closing the extrinsic extended door that leads to a student's external environment. The school's expectations for student learning during an abnormal event need to be communicated to students, teachers, and staff by the principal in a timely manner. Leadership can't wait to exert itself during times that may affect student learning. Leadership must be the front runner in times of crisis. The principal and the administrative staff must be more visible at the school when tragedy strikes. The administrative staff should gather as much information about the situation as possible, monitor the school climate and make decisions accordingly.

There has not been a generation of school-age children that have not been immune to external events, including the generation of students that were in school when I was a public-school student. There probably never will be a group of American students who finish their schooling without being subjected to various types of external events. Some of the events that occurred as I grew up happened when I was in first grade: racial segregation was ruled unconstitutional and Jonas Salk developed the vaccine for polio.

In my ninth grade Martin Luther King gave his "I Have a Dream" speech. President John F. Kennedy was assassinated and Lyndon Baines Johnson became president. There were riots in major cities across the United States when Martin Luther King was assassinated and more disgust when Bobby Kennedy was assassinated. Emotional events occur throughout the twelve to thirteen years when students are enrolled in public and private schools. Such events penetrate a student's mind and soul. Educators are responsible for playing down each major event when the student is in the room of learning.

Extrinsic Limited Breadth: The Learning Room

The Learning Room is where a child's mind opens to receive information from the classroom teacher. A classroom teacher must provide nutritional education for students so they will not suffer from intellectual deficiency. Students learn early in their school years how the major food groups provide nutrients for the body and that without proper nutrition the vital organs and the human body suffers. Students learn that three key components are essential for sustained life: food, water, and oxygen. Oxygen is the vital component because without it, the body will perish within minutes. Students learn that although oxygen is something one cannot see, hear, smell, taste, or feel, life stops without it. Students learn that without food and water humans slowly perish.

There are three educational nutrients that are essential for the sustained development of a child and imperative for a schoolchild's success. There must be purposeful and sound instruction by a competent and well-qualified teacher. Students must have sufficient time to learn and master the essential content at each grade level designed by curriculum planners and approved by the board of education. The blueprint will not succeed unless suitable resources are made available to supplement a child's active learning.

Effective instruction by a highly efficient and organized teacher produces an effect that acts as educational oxygen for the student. It does not take a student long to recognize that they are being taught by a poor teacher and that they will not reach their educational potential with a poor teacher.

Effective teachers provide specific directions for students in the initial meeting at the start of a new course or unit of study. An effective classroom teacher will require a student to carry books, pens, pencils, and paper to all classroom settings. The teacher will demand that the student report to class on time, take a seat and begin work immediately upon entering the classroom. An effective teacher will have learning objectives posted within sight for the student before the student enters the classroom. The student understands the teacher's grading policies and is familiar with the teacher's instructional procedures. An effective teacher explains, discusses and adheres to firm but fair standards of student behavior. A student will not pay attention to the teacher unless the extrinsic extended quadrant has been closed. Otherwise, the student's mind is on something other than the lesson and the teacher.

A poor teacher with weak delivery or management skills will impede their students' attempts to learn and acquire the skills and concepts they need for success. In the end a student who spends considerable time with an ineffective teacher will suffer from a lack of mental stimulation and knowledge. The other two educational nutrients——sufficient time to master essential content and suitable resources for students and teachers——act as food and water. Both educational nutrients are necessary for a student to achieve success in the classroom. Some students are not able to perform at the same pace as fast learners, and they need more time to digest educational content (Oxnard School District, 1992).

The school clock and calendar have governed how material is presented and students must have the opportunity to master the material in a reasonable amount of time. John B. Carroll's *Model of Learning* (1963) identified opportunity to learn as a major factor in school learning. Since there are significant differences in the time it takes students to learn, more time should be provided for slow learners (National Commission on Time and Learning, 1993).

The classroom teacher must instill in children a course of action that is vital for them to take if they expect to be successful. The teacher must be astute and focused on convincing students to find the determination to work hard at learning new concepts. Effective teachers are keen on eliminating reasons why students can't learn even when the students have a difficult background. Teachers are responsible for helping students learn from the mistakes they make, for clarifying what is important to learn and for providing opportunities for students to practice what they have learned to be successful.

During instructional time and student learning the teacher responsible for delivering instruction must establish positive relationships that are nonthreatening to the student. Children prone to negative attitudes during instructional time lack the ability to focus on the teacher and the lesson. These students may appear unhappy and testy in the room of learning, and it becomes difficult for them to transition to the quadrant that is mostly responsible for completing and processing assigned work: the intrinsic limited breadth. The key to student learning lies in the extrinsic limited breadth quadrant controlled by the teacher who must close the door to the extrinsic extended breath quadrant, which is controlled by the student.

Children learn best when teachers capture their attention and make clear what is important to learn without burdening them with unnecessary information. Effective teachers know that without a good background in listening skills, it will be difficult for students to succeed later in life. Active listening means not being distracted by others, by their environment, or by difficulties the speaker may have in getting his or her message across (Rees, 1991). It is very important that the teacher require students to pay attention. If the teacher fails to command attention from all the students before continuing with instruction, the student may determine that the teacher's instruction is not worth listening to. When teachers establish credibility in the classroom they are more likely to capture and hold their students' attention. More importantly, they will enhance their ability to persuade students to follow their instructions (Adler, 1983).

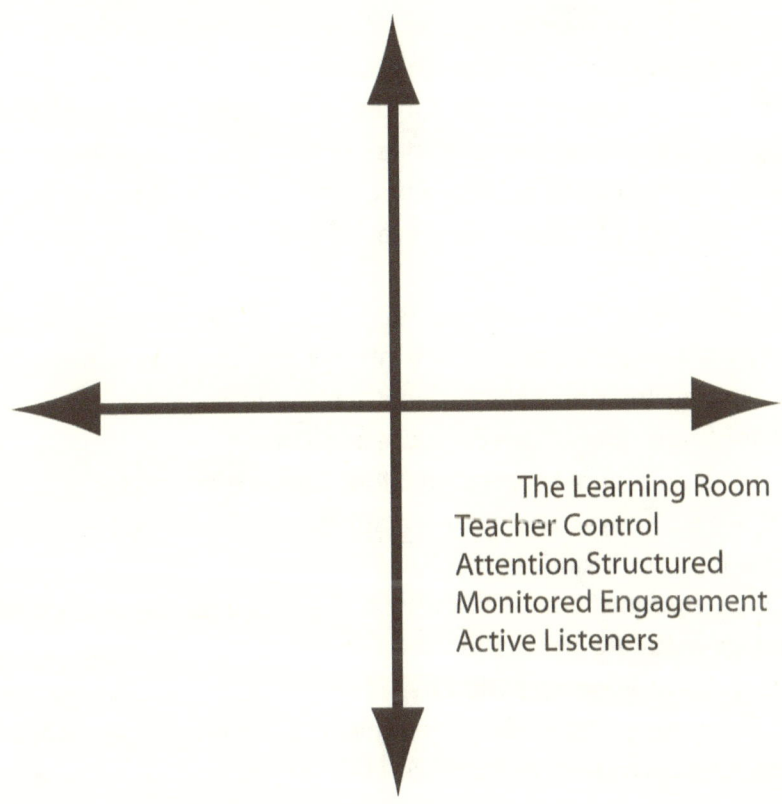

The Learning Room
Teacher Control
Attention Structured
Monitored Engagement
Active Listeners

Teachers should conduct classes with students like defensive car drivers, always aware that other drivers may make mistakes. The teacher should always be on the lookout for the first sign that a student's attention is drifting and stop it before it goes too far (Harming, 1994). Effective teachers know that if the odds are stacked against some schoolchildren, learning is more difficult to achieve. Effective teachers understand the hurdles that confront some students and work diligently to remove obstacles that obstruct learning. The effective teacher helps students to jump over hurdles. Good teachers give relevant examples. They refuse to go well past the student's learning ability. They find passageways that work for students. They continually search for ways to make students productive.

Effective teachers see students as their own children. Therefore they never allow stereotypes to enter their classrooms. Single-parent home, low socioeconomic status, lack of parental involvement, lack of social functions, neglect, danger of dropping out of school, prone to peer pressure, undisciplined, troubled neighborhoods, abusive backgrounds, attention problems, and high risk of failure are never allowed in effective teachers' classrooms.

Effective teachers never enter the classroom seeking a popularity contest because they are always prepared and they never try winging lessons with students because they know the stakes are too high. The best teachers establish a classroom grounded in sound educational principles that prepare the students for the next level. They know how to network with colleagues about ideas that work and with school counselors who know how to change students' social skills. Effective teachers never see a student as a failure no matter what the student's situation is, and they try to provide opportunities for their students to be successful. They are excited about being with children and see hope in every child. Understanding that children learn differently, effective teachers constantly monitor their students' engagement in the lesson to ensure adequate progress. Effective teachers set appropriate expectations for all students. They build strong support systems for their students and are supportive of parents.

Intrinsic Extended Breadth: The Internal Storage Room

Located on the upper left side of the quadrants model is the intrinsic extended breadth quadrant. The intrinsic extended breadth quadrant contains a person's inner mind comprised of the consciousness, memory, intellect, reasoning ability, willpower, understanding, beliefs, imagination, personality, and the ability to make choices. When students deal with external environmental mental pressures the exterior anxiety may lead to conflicts with their internal beliefs. Information taken in through the extrinsic extended and extrinsic limited quadrants is stored in the intrinsic extended breadth quadrant and influences thoughts, feelings, and attitudes.

In the intrinsic extended breadth quadrant the student stores, dissects and examines the information obtained from the extrinsic quadrants. Students distinguish differences between situations under their control (internal) and situations they have no control over (external stimuli). External stimuli such as class work, homework, and state, local and teacher-made tests are under the control of the teacher or someone other than the student. A student may, however, seek control of the situation by making an internal decision to change their study habits. By changing study habits the student may become better organized and prepared for the external stimuli and eventually a better student in school.

Lesson content is external stimulus to be stored in the students' intrinsic extended breadth quadrant. The students' success in the classroom is dependent upon the positive changes they make in their attitude to the work they must accomplish, and upon their understanding that their acceptance of the work will help them succeed. Students with positive attitudes toward schoolwork feel at ease in surroundings characterized by external stimuli and information processing. Abraham Maslow states that attitude may be focused on something in particular or life in general.

Properly internalized decisions made by students in the intrinsic extended breadth quadrant make a difference in how the students react toward the teacher and the lessons taught in the classroom. A student who displays positive attitudes in class and accepts the information presented by the teacher is able to retrieve stored information from the intrinsic extended breadth quadrant much more easily.

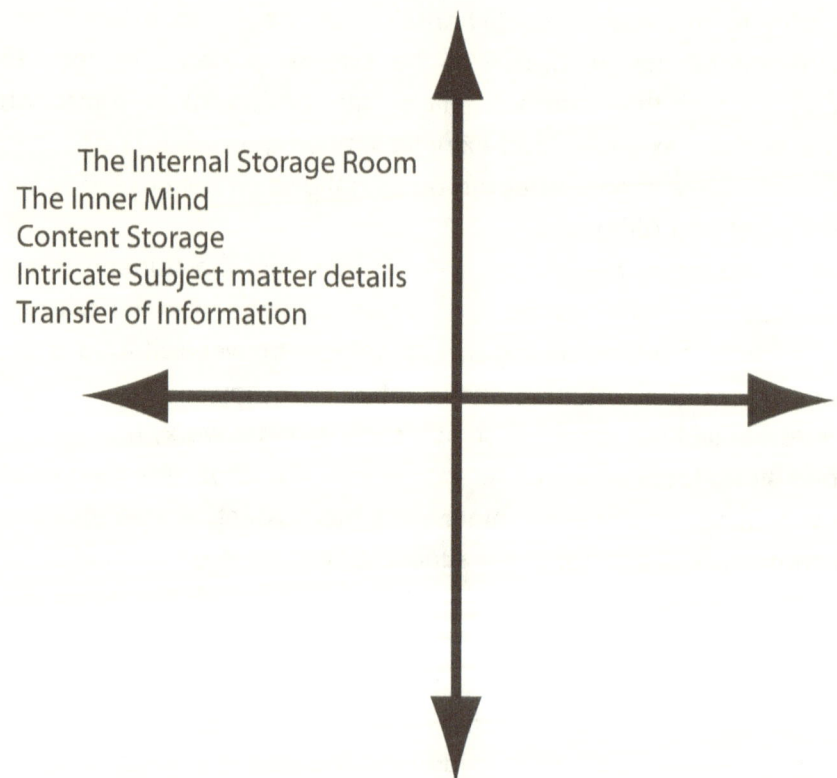

The Internal Storage Room
The Inner Mind
Content Storage
Intricate Subject matter details
Transfer of Information

It is at the intrinsic extended breadth quadrant that a student's willpower to learn and succeed emerges. The preparatory process of storing information related to specific content takes place in the student's intrinsic extended breadth quadrant. Intricate details of information communicated by teachers during instructional time or generated by the student and accurately stored in the intrinsic extended breadth quadrant can easily be retrieved when needed by the student. When the student's attention focuses on the teacher and the lesson the student is assured that all the teacher's instructions will be stored appropriately. There will be no problem in recovering information from the storage room to complete overnight work, homework, reading and writing assignments, or class projects within a set timeframe if accomplished the right way.

The number of assignments students must fulfill affects whether they decide to devote themselves to leisure time in the extrinsic extended breadth quadrant or complete the assignments. The assignment could be long term. It could be a science project or term paper that may take several days or weeks to complete. The student must review the details of the long-term assignment and decide when and how much time to devote to the project. The information acquired in the learning room——the extrinsic limited breadth quadrant——and uploaded into the storage room——the intrinsic extended breadth quadrant——must be secured before the extrinsic extended breath quadrant——the outside door——opens, unless it is opened for the purpose of retrieving relevant information connected to the lesson. The students' ability to act upon images from the extrinsic extended breadth quadrant does not interfere with their ability to process information later on if they have transferred the teacher's information to the intrinsic extended breadth in a timely manner. Students must store information in the intrinsic extended breadth quadrant soon after an interaction with the teacher.

The amount of time devoted to long-term assignments is critical for the success of the project. When students make a decision to complete assignments immediately after receiving the coursework more time is available for extrinsic extended breadth activities. Completing assignments early prevents the feeling of being rushed. Some students decide to work on long-term assignments intermittently, splitting time between the intrinsic extended, the intrinsic limited, the extrinsic limited, and the extrinsic extended breadth quadrants. Some students decide to work on long-term assignments at the last moment. In this case they close the intrinsic extended breadth quadrant, the intrinsic limited breadth quadrant, and the extrinsic limited breadth quadrant and spend time in the extrinsic extended breadth quadrant. As the deadline for the assignment nears, students who wait until the last moment to complete the long-term project must scuttle between the three essential quadrants——the extended limited, the intrinsic extended, and the intrinsic limited breadth quadrant——with little time for external enjoyment.

Regardless of when a student decides to finish an assignment, he or she must journey between the extrinsic limited quadrant (what the teacher delivered), the intrinsic extended quadrant (how the information was stored) and the intrinsic limited breadth quadrants (information processing). The transfer of information from one quadrant to another occurs the moment work is assigned by the teacher. The process continues until the student completes the work and hands over the finished product to the teacher. The student's decision to complete an assignment starts at the extrinsic limited breadth quadrant. All of the parameters set by the teacher are acquired in the extrinsic limited quadrant, the learning room, and delivered to the intrinsic extended quadrant.

When a teacher sets the parameters for completion of an assignment——a writing assignment, for instance——the student must store in the intrinsic extended breadth quadrant information that determines the length of the writing assignment, the number of words or pages, the format, whether typed or handwritten, whether a pencil, pen, or word processor is used, the ink color, the spacing——single or double——and the due date or other qualifiers. Writing down key aspects of the parameters as the teacher explains the information is vital for the successful completion of the project. Teachers should require students to take notes in class. Giving students handouts instead of having students take notes in class supplants the flow of information to the intrinsic extended quadrant and does not allow the student to reach higher levels of learning. Benjamin S. Bloom recorded six cognitive domains from the lowest to highest level of learning; knowledge, comprehension, application, analysis, synthesis, and evaluation. When students are challenged to construct, categorize, compose and choose they are given chances to elevate their learning. Success in the classroom requires students to transfer parameters set by teachers directly to the intrinsic extended breadth quadrant in an opportune manner.

Intrinsic Limited Breadth: The Processing Room

The intrinsic limited breadth quadrant, the processing room, is the central room where learned and stored information from the intrinsic extended breadth quadrant is sorted out by the student. Students must conceptualize, compile, separate and package the content information when it is requested by the teacher. Appropriately stored information allows the student to retrieve information without undue stress. Information that is not captured by the student cannot be stored and if it is not stored, the information cannot be processed.

Successful and effective teachers expect children to learn and they are surprised when students fall short of success in their classroom. Poor teachers, on the other hand, are not amazed when students are unsuccessful. If poor teachers were asked to name children likely to fail in their classes, they would readily name a number of students. Poor teachers have low expectations for some students because they have a difficult time capturing the attention of their students. They lack the ability to close their students' external mental doors, which is necessary for success. Poor teachers place the blame for failure on the students instead of on themselves. The inability of teachers to capture their students' attention reduces their students' ability to store and process information.

In the intrinsic limited breadth quadrant students set in motion the process of connecting information stored in the intrinsic extended breadth quadrant. This is a critical phase in the learning process because student success depends on the student's ability to return information requested by teachers.

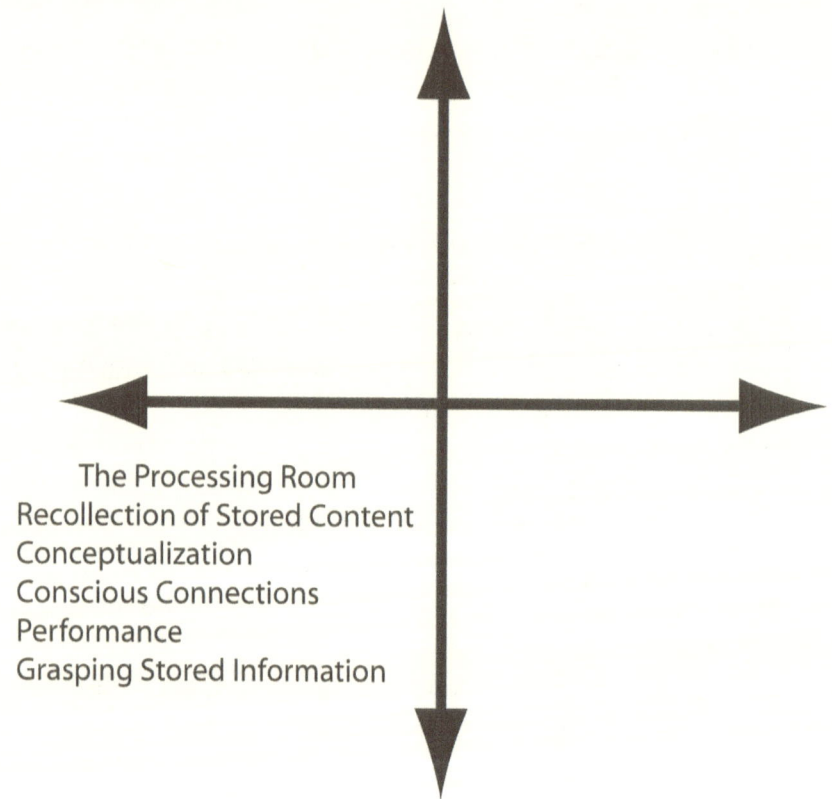

The Processing Room
Recollection of Stored Content
Conceptualization
Conscious Connections
Performance
Grasping Stored Information

Processing information necessitates elaborate coordination between three quadrants of the model: the extrinsic limited, intrinsic extended, and intrinsic limited breadth quadrants. When the student is in the processing room it is time for the student to perform. The student undertakes a series of consciously connected actions from the bottom right to the upper and bottom left quadrants. The philosopher Emmanuel Kant reasoned that one cannot infer new relationships among objects, events, or actions unless one has an established viewpoint through which perceptions can be organized. This viewpoint affects how one makes sense of new information.

The student grasps information stored in the intrinsic extended quadrant and internalizes it in the intrinsic limited quadrant. The information is then used in the intrinsic limited quadrant to complete self-imposed or externally imposed tasks. Recollection of information is essentially an introspective act. John Dewey (1966) refers to introspection as, "an alleged act of immediate and intuitive knowledge of mind or of consciousness."

Information is stored in the students' intrinsic extended breadth quadrant and then loaded into the students' intrinsic limited quadrant for analysis or the completion of a task.

The Individual Quadrants for Success Model

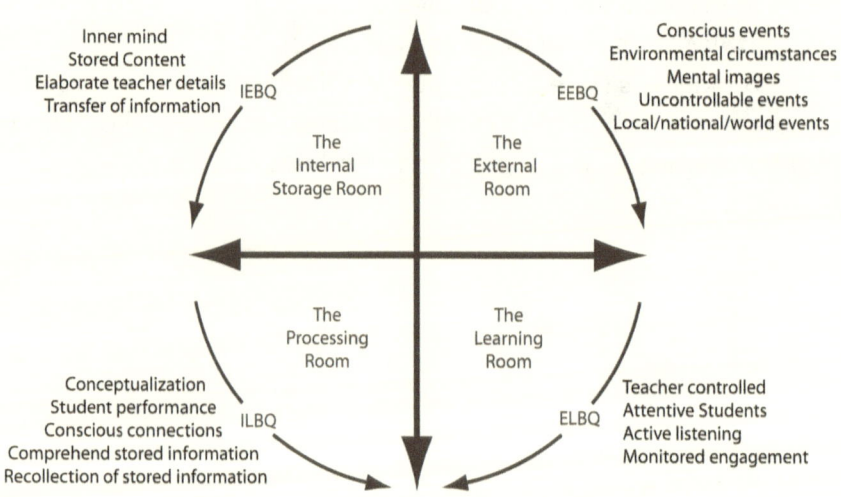

Inner mind
Stored Content
Elaborate teacher details
Transfer of information

IEBQ

EEBQ

Conscious events
Environmental circumstances
Mental images
Uncontrollable events
Local/national/world events

The
Internal
Storage Room

The
External
Room

The
Processing
Room

The
Learning
Room

Conceptualization
Student performance
Conscious connections
Comprehend stored information
Recollection of stored information

ILBQ

ELBQ

Teacher controlled
Attentive Students
Active listening
Monitored engagement

CHAPTER 7

Role of Parents: Prior to Formal Education

Parents are involved in their children's education from birth. They develop a culture from the moment children are born. They teach family values and practices, traditions, customs, culture, and the family life before their children enter the formal education process. Parents are children's first teachers. They teach family culture through a process of enculturation. Enculturation, the informal education of children, continues until the children enroll in school for its formal education. The sound nurturing of children by parents will create a positive feeling in the children at school.

Children who feel secure at home adjust to school better than children who are insecure in their home life. Children who feel secure explore their external surroundings more easily. Their exploration of their surroundings depends on the attractiveness of their environment. Children who live in deplorable neighborhoods may not feel safe exploring those neighborhoods. Lack of exploration becomes a detriment to the natural growth and development of children.

Parents or guardians who raise children during their earliest years are the children's primary teachers. They impart language, knowledge, and standards to their children. The values that parents convey to children are important to later success in school and life. If parental values are supportive of schooling, the teacher can build on these predispositions. If parental attitudes are negative to schooling, children's attitudes are also likely to be negative (Gutek, 1988).

Public schools and school districts recently received legislative mandates requiring them to find creative ways to include parents and the community in school functions. Schools are encouraged to include a comprehensive parent-involvement program as part of their school involvement plan. Prior to state mandated parent-involvement initiatives, parents were less involved in school functions. Schools continue to have legal responsibility for children. As ruled by the courts, they act in place of the parent——*in loco parentis*. *In loco parentis* allows schools the rights of biological parents when children are away from their parents and in the care of the school.

Parental involvement has always been a natural part of the educational process and serves as a valuable resource for schools. Parents serve on PTA boards and committees. They are a part of the school improvement team. They attend school conferences, chaperone field trips, help with celebrations, attend workshops, work in classrooms, attend school assemblies, visit their children's classes, and volunteer their time and energy. Public schools and teachers must keep parents informed of their children's educational progress. Parents are encouraged to stay involved in their children's education.

References

Adler, M. J. 1984. *The Paideia Program: An Educational Syllabus.* New York: MacMillan Publishing Company.

Alcorn, R. D. 1992. "Test Scores: Can Year-Round School Raise Them?" *Thrust for Educational Leadership* 21: 12–15.

Armstrong, D. G., and T. V. Savage. 1983. *Secondary Education: An Introduction.* New York: MacMillan Publishing Company.

Ballinger, C. 1995. *The Year-Round Education in Review.* San Diego, California: National Association for Year Round Education.

Ballinger, C. 1996. *A Preview: The Year-Rounder* 23: 1-10. San Diego, California: National Association for Year Round Education.

Beck, J. 1992. "The Learning Gap Between Asian and U. S. Schools." *The Chicago Tribune*: April 20.

Bennett, W. J. 1986. "First Lessons: A Report on Elementary Education in America." Washington, D.C.: U.S Department of Education.

Bruner, J. S. 1963. "Structures in Learning." *Today's Education.* (March).

Campbell, R. F., J. E. Corbally, and R. O. Nystrand. 1983. *Introduction to Educational Administration*. Newton, Massachusetts: Allyn & Bacon.

Carroll, J. B. 1963. "A Model of School Learning." *Teachers College Record*.

Cartwright, D., and A. Zander. 1963. *Group Dynamics: Research and Theory*. New York: Harper & Row.

Cetron, M., and M. Gayle. 1991. *Educational Renaissance: Our Schools at the Turn of the Century*. New York: St. Martin's Press.

Covey, S. R. 1992. *Principle-Centered Leadership*. New York: Simon & Schuster.

Covey, S. R. 1990. *The 7 Habits of Highly Effective People*. New York: Simon & Schuster.

Daggett, W. A. 1990. "Demographics of American Workplace: Future Workplace Is Shocking." *North Carolina Education Journal*, North Carolina Association of Education._

Dewey, J. 1966. *Philosophy of Education (Problems of Men)*. Totowa, New Jersey: Littlefield, Adams and Company.

Dlugosh, L. L. 1993. "Quality Schools and the Myth of the Nine-Month School Year." (April). Paper presented at the Annual University of Oklahoma National Conference on Creating the Quality School (Norman, Oklahoma).

Drake, T. L., and w. H. Roe. 1986. *The Principalship*, 3rd ed. New York, New York: Macmillan Publishing Company.

Eisner, E. W. 1991. *The Enlightened Eye*. New York: MacMillan Publishing Company.

Elmore R. F. and S. H. Fuhrman. 1994. *The Governance of Curriculum*.

Alexandria, Virginia: Association for Supervision and Curriculum Development.

First, P. F. 1992. *Educational Policy for School Administrators*. Needham Heights, Massachusetts: Allyn & Bacon.

First, P. F., and H. J. Walberg. 1992. *Schools Boards: Changing Local Control*. Berkeley, California: McCutchan Publishing Corporation

Fraenkel, J. R. and N. E. Wallen. 1993. *How to Design and Evaluate Research in Education*. New York: McGraw-Hill.

Fullan, M.G. 1993. *Change Forces: Probing the Depths of Educational Reform*. New York: The Falmer Press.

Gandara, P. and J. Fish. 1994. "Year-Round Schooling as an Avenue to Major Structural Reform." *Educational Evaluation and Policy Analysis* Vol.16: 67-85.

Gates, K. E. and B. Fass-Holmes. 1994. "Report on Single Track Year-Round Education in San Diego Unified School District." San Diego, California: San Diego Unified School District.

Gentile, R. J. 1988. *Instructional Improvement: Summary & Analysis of Madeline Hunter's Essential Elements of Instruction & Supervision*. Oxford, Ohio: National Staff Development Council.

Glass, G. V. 1992. "Policy Considerations in Conversion to Year-Round Schools." *Policy Briefs*. Education Policy Studies Laboratory.

Glasser, W. 1992. *The Quality School: Managing Students Without Coercion*. New York: HarperCollins Publishers, Inc.

Glickman, C. D., S. P. Gordon, and J. M. Ross-Gordon. 1995. *Supervision of Instruction: A Developmental Approach*. Needham Heights, Massachusetts: Simon & Schuster.

Glickman, C. D. 1990. *Supervision of Instruction: A Developmental Approach*, 2nd ed. Needham, Heights, Massachusetts: Allyn & Bacon.

Glines, D. 1996. *National Association for Year-Round Education: Understanding YRE Basics*. San Diego, Calif.: National Association for Year-Round Education.

Goodlad, J. I. 1984. *A Place Called School*. New York: McGraw-Hill.

Greenfield, T. A. 1994. "Year-Round Education: A Case for Change." *Educational Forum* 58: 252-262.

Greenfield, W. 1987. *Instructional Leadership: Concepts, Issues, and Controversies.* Newton, Massachusetts: Allyn & Bacon.

Gutek, G. L. 1988. *Education and Schooling in America,* 2nd ed. Englewood Cliffs, New Jersey: Prentice Hall.

Harming, M. 1994. *Inspiring Active Learning: A Handbook for Teachers.* Alexandria, Virginia: Association for Supervision and Curriculum Development.

Harp, L. 1993. "Advocates of Year-Round Schooling Shift Focus to Educational Benefits." *Education Week: February 24.*

Hass, G., and F. W. Parkay. 1993. *Curriculum Planning: A New Approach, Sixth Edition.* Needham Heights, Massachusetts: Allyn & Bacon.

Herman, J. 1991. "Novel Approaches to Relieve Over-Crowding: The Effects of Concept on Six Year-Round Schools." *Urban Education* Vol.26: 195-213.

Hoff, D. J. 1997. "Clinton Gives Top Billing to Education Plan." *Education Week* (February 12): 1-32.

Hunter, M. 1982. *Improved Instruction.* El Segundo, California: TIP Publications.

Kegan, R. 1994. *In Over Our Heads: The Mental Demand of Modern Life.* Cambridge, Mass.: Harvard Press.

Kilpatrick, W. H. 1941. "The Case for Progressivism in Education." *Today's Education: Journal of the National Education Association* (November 1941).

Knox, G. 1994. "Seven Rules to Year-Round Schooling." *School Administrator* 51: 22-24.

Kouzes, J.M. and B. Z. Posner. 1987. *The Leadership Challenge.* San Francisco, Calif.: Jossey-Bates, Inc.

Lawyer, E.R. 1986. *High Involvement Management.* San Francisco, Calif.: Jossey-Bates, Inc.

Letteri, C. A. 1985. "Teaching Students How to Learn." *Theoryinto Practice* (Spring): 113.

Lezotte, L. 1994. "The Nexus of Instructional Leadership and Effective Schools." *School Administrator* 51: 20-23.

Lezotte, L. and J. C. Pepperl. 2004. *Instructional Leadership: What the Effective Research Says.* Okemos, Michigan.

Loyd, C. R. 1991. *Crockett Intermediate School Study of Retention of Learning.* Conroe, Texas: Conroe Independent School District.

Maine Task Force on Year-Round Education. 1994. *Rethinking the School Calendar.* Augusta, Maine: Maine State Department of Education.

McCall, J. R. 1988. *The Provident Principal.* Chapel Hill, North Carolina: Institute of Government, University of North Carolina.

McCoy, T. M. 1991. *Curriculum Alignment.* Fayetteville, North Carolina: Cumberland County Schools:

Milton, J., P. Hlustik, S. L. Small and A. Solodkin. 2007. *The Mind of Expert Motor Performance is Cool and Focused.* Chicago, Illinois: Department of Neurology and Brain Research Imaging Center, The University of Chicago.

Mizell, M. H. 1995. *The New Principal: Risk, Reform, and the Quest for Hard Core Learning.* Louisville, Kentucky: Middle School Principal Institute.

Morgan, G. 1986. *Images of Organizations.* Newbury Park, Calif.: Sage Publications, Inc.

Naour, P. 1985. "Brain/Behavior Relationships, Gender Differences, and the Learning Disabled." *Theory into Practice* (Spring).

National Association of Secondary Schools Principals. 1994. *Leadership in Middle Level Education.* Reston, Virginia.

National Commission on Excellence in Education. 1983. *A Nation at Risk: The Imperative for Educational Reform.* Washington, D.C.: U. S. Government Printing Office.

National Education Commission on Time and Learning. 1993. *Hearing of the National Education Commission on Time and Learning Summary.* Washington, D. C.: U.S. Department of Education.

National Middle School Association. 1977. *The Middle School: A Look Ahead*. Gainesville, Florida: University of Florida

New York State Board of Regents. 1992. *Learning Loss Study*. New York.

North Carolina Department of Public Instruction. 1993. *North Carolina End of Grade Testing Program*. Raleigh, N.C.: Division of Accountability Services.

North Carolina State Board of Education. 1994. *Public School Laws of North Carolina*. Raleigh, N.C.: Michie Company.

Oliva, P. F. 1988. *Developing the Curriculum*, 2nd ed. Brown College Division. Glenview, Illinois: Scott, Foresman and Company.

Oxnard School District. 1992. *What YRE Can Do to Enhance Academic Achievement to Enrich the Lives of Students that the Calendar Cannot Do*. Oxnard, California: Oxnard School District.

Paslay, B. 1992. *Conventional and Year-Round Program 60-20 Plan Comparison*. Texarkana, Texas: Texarkana Independent School District.

Powers, D. 1974. *The Virginia Beach Extended School Year program and Its Effects on Student Achievement and Attitudes: First Year Report*. Princeton, New Jersey: Educational Testing Service.

Raspberry, Q. 1994. "Research Summary: Year-Round Schools May Not Be the Answer." Paper presented at the Conference for Private Child Care Centers and Preschool (Orlando, Florida).

Rees, F. 1991. *How to Lead Work Teams: Faciliation Skills*. San Diego, Calif.: Pfeiffer & Company.

Riechman, D. 1996. "Report Card Scores Stay Flat Over Years: No Drastic Changes Nationwide." *Charlotte Observer* (October): A6.

Rodgers and Hammerstein. 1982. "Climb Ev'ry Mountain" from *The Sound Of Music*. The Don Shirley Trio (CBS, Inc.). Silver BurdettCompany.

Rosenthal, R. and R. L. Rosnow. 1991. *Essentials of Behavioral Research: Methods and Data Analysis.* New York: McGraw-Hill.

Ross, R. A. 1989. *Small Groups in Organizational Settings.* Englewood Cliffs: New Jersey: Prentice Hall.

Rothberg, R. A. and G. E. Pawlas. 1993. *Leadership for Structured Schools: What Is Necessary?* Reston, Virginia: NAASP.

Senge, P. M. 1993. "Transforming the Practice of Management." *Human Resource Development Quarterly.* Vol.4 Spring:5-32.

Sergiovanni, T. J. 1992. *Moral Leadership: Getting to the Heart of School Improvement.* San Francisco, Calif.: Jossey-Bates, Inc.

Shepherd, G.D. and W. B. Ragan. 1982. *Modern Elementary Curriculum.* Orlando, Fl: Holt, Rinehart and Winston, Inc.

Smith, W. F. and R. L. Andrews. 1989. *Instructional Leadership: How Principals Make a Difference.* Alexandria, Virginia: Association for Supervision and Curriculum Development.

Sousa, D. A. 1995. *How the Brain Learns.* Reston, Virginia: The National Association of Secondary Schools Principals. State Board of Education. 1993. Principals' Executive Program, University of North Carolina, Chapel Hill.

State Board of Education. 2003. *Public School Laws of North Carolina.* Charlottesville, Virginia: Matthew Bender & Company.

Summerfield, M. 1993. "Time and Space." *Education Week* 4: 13-19.

The Commission on the Bicentennial of the United States Constitution. 1986.

The Constitution of the United States and the Declaration of Independence. Washington, D. C.

Thompson, J. 199). *Modified School Calendar Program 1992-93 Results.* Jacksonville, Fl.: Duval County Public Schools.

Tocci, C.M. and G. Engelhart. 1991. "Achievement, Parental Support, and Gender Differences in Attitudes Toward Mathematics." *Journal of Educational Research* 84: 281-285.

Virginia State Department of Education. 1992. *Instructional Time and Learning: A Study of the School Calendar and Instructional Time*. Richmond, Virginia.

Walton, M. 1986. *The Deming Management Method*. New York: Perigee Books.

Webb, D. L., M. M. McCarthy, and S. B. Thomas. 1988. *Financing Elementary and Secondary Education*. Columbus, Ohio: Merrill Publishing Company.

Webb, R. B. 1981. *Schooling and Society*. New York: Macmillan Publishing Company.

Wiebe, D. J. 1992. "Restructuring Through a New School Calendar." *School Administrator* 4: 30.

Winters, W. L. 1994. *A Review of Recent Studies Relating to the Achievement of Students Enrolled in Year-Round Education Programs*. San Diego, Calif.: National Association for Year-Round Education.

Worthen, B. R. and S. W. Zsivay. 1994. *What Twenty Years of Educational Studies Reveal about Year-Round Education*. Chapel Hill, North Carolina: North Carolina Educational Policy Research Center, University of North Carolina.

Yukl, G. 1994. *Leadership in Organizations*. Englewood Cliffs, New Jersey: Prentice Hall.